# Opening a Closed Door:

# A Psychotherapist Remembers His Patients

## Alexander Boeringa, PhD, ABPP

To my wonderful sons, Michael Alexander

and Matthew David, for the joy you bring

to my life.

# I.  CONTENTS

**II.  INTRODUCTION 7**

**III.  FIRST CASES 11**

   A.  The Cleaning Lady 12
   B.  The Cement Truck Driver 15
   C.  Welcome to the "Nam" 19
   D.  Inner Adult to the Rescue 22
   E.  Unhappy Anniversary 26
   F.  Blushing 30
   G.  The Hallway Walker 35
   H.  The Hypnotic Doctor B? 37
   I.  Other Examples 41

**IV.  DIFFERENT STROKES 44**

   A.  A Needle Phobic 46
   B.  Rhona 50
   C.  John 54
   D.  Mrs. Pluedine 57
   E.  Let's All Play Uproar 61
   F.  Yakety Yak, Take out the Trash 64
   G.  The Man Who Cried 67
   H.  I Love You 71
   I.  The Car Loan 74
   J.  The Whiners 78

**V.  THE FUN ONES 82**

   A.  My First Patient 83
   B.  A Day's Outing 87

C.   Wilma 89
D.   The Prostitute's New Life 92
E.   Never Trust a Little Old Lady 95
F.   Junior 98
G.   My Very Own Gang 100
H.   Pick-Up Sticks 103
I.   The Other Side of the Street 108

## VI.   THE YOUNG ONES 112

A.   Give Kids a Chance 113
B.   Motorcycle Lady 117
C.   The Actor 119
D.   Look at Me 121
E.   The Doctor 124
F.   Toilet Training 126

## VII.   THE SEXY ONES 131

A.   Honesty 133
B.   Beth 136
C.   Trust 139
D.   How Many Times? 142
E.   Never Too Old 144
F.   Not So Gay 145
G.   Ted's Story 148
H.   A Good Catholic Man 150
I.   The Sex Therapist 153

## VIII. THE SCARY ONES 155

A.   Charles Whitman 156
B.   Tick Tock 158
C.   The Sunrise 160
D.   The Stone-Cold Killer? 163
E.   Walking Bird 165

F.    Secret Agent Man 168

G.   Guns 170

## IX.   THE SAD ONES 172

A.   The Wild Boy 173

B.   Carole Lee 176

C.   The Three Graces 179

D.   Ronny 181

E.   The Dream Girl 184

## X.   DEALING WITH DEATH 187

A.   The Red Truck 190

B.   The Grave Problem 193

C.   The Man Who Raised Me 195

D.   Coping with Suicides 197

E.   A Suicide Pact 199

## XI.   THE ONES I LOVED MOST 201

A.   Cinderella 202

B.   One of My Heroes 204

C.   Joe 206

D.   Two Beautiful Boys 208

E.   I Remember Them 211

F.   Clyde 214

G.   A Closing Note on this Chapter 216

## XII.  THE ONE ABOUT ME 217

A.   Alexander 219

B.   A Premature Postscript 223

C.   Other Duties as Assigned 224

    1.   Employee Assistance 226

    2.   Mediation 229

    3.   Grief Counseling 231

4.   ER Duty 233
5.   False Positives/Negatives 236
6.   Testifying 238
7.   Workshops and Mandated Training Seminars 240

**XIII. CONCLUSION 243**

**XIV. APPENDIX 245**

A.   Nuts and Bolts 245
1.   How Psychotherapy Works: I Don't Know 246
How Psychotherapy Works: What I DO Know 248
2.   A Few Things I Have Learned the Hard Way 249
3.   Confidentiality: Ask but Don't Tell 252
4.   Same and Different 254
B.   Alexander's Rules of the Road 256
C.   A Few Paraphrased Quotes from Literature 260

# II. INTRODUCTION

The people in this book are the ones that keep coming to mind even many years later and crowded my thoughts as I wrote. In a way, they would not be denied. Some mornings I woke up with a memory almost fully formed in my consciousness and I had to write it down. There are, of course, many others' stories. They will just have to wait. Even so, I have given a great deal of thought both to the cases I included, and those I excluded. I have my reasons for choosing each of them. The best explanation for these selections has already been made by my friend and colleague Deirdre Barrett, PhD. In the introduction to *The Pregnant Man* she writes:

> How did I choose which patient's stories to include? Occasionally, therapy unfolds like a play, with me at times audience, at other times actor, but never holding more than a fragment of the script. A colorful character walks in and presents a problem, there are several unexpected twists in the plot, and a solution arrives climactically (or fails climactically...).

To expand on this, the stories I have chosen are the ones which, in the process of therapy, have opened up something in me. The patients in these stories have enhanced my life and changed it. Their problems deal with universal human issues. The manner in which people coming from diverse viewpoints and backgrounds confront their issues in different ways has helped me, as well as them, to learn and grow as human beings. If there is some myth

7

that psychotherapists (or parents, teachers, ministers, priests, rabbis, imams, etc.) somehow have it all together, have confronted all their devils, know all the answers and are healthy in all respects, let me disabuse the lie. I for one still have a long way to go.

In some cases I have struggled with issues similar to those of my patients. Often their progress encouraged me to face my own life problems. At other times I could admire the tremendous courage it took to confront difficult and at times horrendous experiences. Each of these people has in some way helped to "cure" me in the process of my helping them.

Necessary cautions: This is not a scholarly work, nor is it intended to be. It is *not* a how-to-do-it book, a self-help guide, or a "Psychotherapy for Dumb-Dumbs" book. Clearly put, it does not qualify you to intervene in someone else's life. It can, however, be useful in the classroom as it introduces students to actual therapy cases, something they may seldom encounter elsewhere. The people and cases I write about are all real but I have, of course, protected their identities as well as I can. In some cases I combined similar traits or therapies into those of one person or added minor fictional elements to disguise them. I trust that the fiction never overcomes the truth and the core remains the reality.

In referring to people I saw, I most often use "patient" rather than "client" or "customer," and "therapy" rather than "counseling." Often the terms can be interchangeable; I use the ones that I am most comfortable with. This does not imply that the patients were necessarily sick in a medical sense, only that they sought to make a change in their life and looked for healing.

I think that I must belong to that group of people who seem to have "You can talk to me" written on their foreheads. Not only talk to me, but also tell me the kinds of things that one does not usually tell strangers; or anyone else for that matter. They may chose to do this during a brief encounter in a checkout line, at a cocktail party, or while I am trapped in the seat next to them on a trans-Atlantic flight. Some people who receive this kind of uninvited emotional encounter just accept it and shrug it off. They may not even be aware that these things do not happen to everyone. I made my life profession out of it.

Before I became a card-carrying, educationally ordained, and licensed clinical psychologist, I went through a few "real life" experiences along the way. I spent two years in the Army, graduated from college, worked on a garbage truck and as a plumber and a few other sidelines, including trying my hand as a hippie. I went to graduate school, but was kicked out. It was the Sixties. In 1974, I finally returned to graduate school, and this time exited with a PhD in Clinical Psychology.

My first professional job was as faculty at a medical school. During that time I had married and when my first child was born, I decided that I needed to choose between being a father (as I conceived of the responsibilities) and a full professor with tenure in a publish-or-perish career track. I am sure others can do both admirably, but I made the right choice for me: I changed occupations. I worked for the Veterans Administration (VA) and over several years rose through the ranks to become more of an administrator than a full-time clinician. I still saw patients, some in private practice, taught part-time in a variety of settings, gave occasional lectures and seminars, supervised students, and published a few articles in professional journals. After many years, I retired from the VA. For the next ten years, I taught undergraduate psychology and graduate counseling classes for the University of Maryland Overseas Program on various military bases in Europe. This allowed me to travel a lot. I am now again retired.

I encourage you to read this book in any order you like, page through it, or begin by reading the Appendix at the end. It is now your book.

# III.    FIRST CASES

The section headings are often not precise and there may be a Procrustean bed quality to them. Not everything fits neatly into a category. These are the cases that first came to mind and they are a mixed lot, but in the end I trusted my intuition and followed the advice of James Thurber: "Don't get it right, just get it written."

I once asked Dr. Harry Goolishian, a supervisor of mine, what the essence of therapy was.[1] He told me that it was like unraveling a sweater: You just start somewhere then pick one string and keep pulling at it. I must have looked confused because he elaborated and told me that to unbalance a wheel you just need to remove one of the spokes. I think I got it then. There is a lot more to therapy than this, but any change can be the beginning of change. The point is to begin: So let us begin.

---

[1] Harold A. Goolishian (1924-1991), one of the founders of the Houston Galveston Institute, was my supervisor in Family Therapy and one of my sponsors for the Diploma in Clinical Psychology, ABPP.

ABPP represents  Diplomat in Clinical Psychology, Board Certified by the American Board of Professional Psychology.

## A.   The Cleaning Lady

When I was doing my practicum training at the University of Texas at Austin Student Health Center, many students presented with problems of relationships and intimacy as well as coping with what we call "separation/individuation" issues with their parents. One of the students I saw fell in the latter category. I could see her in the waiting room, tall and a little slouched over, she approached shyly when I called her name. She was a young woman in her freshman year who described her reason for the visit as having what she referred to as "independence issues." I asked her to tell me about these.

It seems that her mother, who lived in Houston, insisted that Sandra show her all of her test scores and she wanted to see a copy of Sandra's grades on an ongoing basis. Her mother would call almost nightly to make sure that Sandra was at home studying and would ask about each of her classes. In addition, the mother had demanded a key to her apartment, "since after all she was paying for it," and since Houston is so close she would frequently show up unannounced and uninvited.

Remembering the advice to pull at any string to get the ball rolling, I asked what bugged her most. That was easy: No matter how clean and orderly Sandra kept her small apartment, when her mother visited she would clean it thoroughly before Sandra got home. Just in case the activity was missed there would always be a strong odor of bleach and other cleaning fluids left behind. Then her mother would complain about what a mess it had been and say that she didn't know what her daughter would do without her-- for the "thousandth time." Now you do not have to be very psychologically sophisticated to interpret some of this, but their total mother-daughter relationship was not the focus that Sandra had requested.

Enter Paradoxical Intention--our useful friend from the last case--or what might in lay terms be called reverse psychology. I suggested that in the future Sandra leave the apartment moderately unclean and have a few things noticeably lying around as if she had forgotten or neglected to put them away. Then she was to go to the store and amass several varieties of cleaning supplies in addition to those she had already. These should include window-washing materials, floor wax and toilet cleaners that were all to be put in one obvious place. A prominently displayed note for her mother was to mention that she had been too busy and would her mommy dearest mind "cleaning up just a little bit?" And by the way the bathroom had been neglected recently and the windows were just a little dusty. Rather that resent the cleaning as before she was to demand that her mother do this for her.

Nothing happened the first week and things were much the same between her mother and her, but when Sandra returned for her next appointment, she was very excited. When she returned home the previous Friday, her mother's car was in the front of the apartment and inside she found her mother on the couch reading. The cleaning supplies were untouched and the note was in the same place it was when she left. Not a word was spoken about any of these items and her mother almost immediately suggested that they go out to dinner. The weekend continued to pass pleasantly with no mention made of "the elephant in the room." Surprisingly for once there were no questions asked about grades and the mother mostly talked about the possibility of going on a vacation cruise with a friend of hers and a little gossip about how the neighbors seemed to be getting a divorce. They had a pleasant walk through Barton

Springs Park and went to a movie together that both had wanted to see. Still no hint that the cleaning supplies or prominent note even existed.

During our session, Sandra was all giggles as she recounted this and, probably for effect, exaggerated the messiness of the apartment, the quantity of the things she had bought and the acting on the part of her mother in pretending to ignore everything so completely. Then she said the best part was that as her mother was leaving on Sunday afternoon she casually remarked that she did not want to scold but that she thought that it was high time that Sandra assume more adult responsibility; she could not take care of her forever. With that, she got in the car and drove off.

Sandra was able to relate that she felt very pleased with the outcome. She felt better about herself and at the same time surprisingly more affectionate towards her mother. An office checkup one month later found Sandra much more in charge of her own life, but able to admit that she had been "a little" dependent before. The frequency of her mother's visits decreased, but they were much more pleasant. Not a word was ever said about the note or cleaning materials.

I do not think that this ploy would be effective in every situation, but in this case the mix seemed to be just right and it probably contributed that both parties were evidently ready to make changes in their relationship. I could not have known this of course but, as in so many seat-of-the-pants hunches, this was a high-reward and low-risk gamble that worked out quite well.

Sandra is old enough by now to have her own daughter; I wonder how their relationship has been?

14

## B.    The Cement Truck Driver

Everyone knows, or thinks they know, what a phobia is. After all there has been a lot of media attention surrounding phobias and many fictional characterizations of it in movies such as *Arachnophobia*. If a person expresses a fear of something, they will almost inevitably be asked if they have a phobia. Googling several popular web sites would have you believe that there are hundreds of phobias all individualized with their own names and the incidence in the population might be as high as 50%. I have "phobophobia" or fear of made up names for phobias, and think that these are mostly disinformation useful only for amusement. Skipping the full lecture, I would say that phobias do exist, are a subset of anxiety disorders, consist of strong fears that the person knows are irrational, and they interfere significantly with daily activities. A bad experience can cause you to avoid even the possibility of it happening again and the fear can grow to control almost every aspect of your life. You have learned to be afraid. This is what happened to Arnold.

My patient Arnold had been a cement truck driver in a small town in Illinois for several years. As he sat in my office I thought that with his short hair, reddish face, and stocky build with thick arms and large hands, he even looked like the stereotype of a brawny truck driver. As he told me his story, the tough guy image began to slowly fade. His hands trembled slightly and from time to time he wiped away a tear with his sleeve. I know that it is a cliché, but I began to feel the pain he was experiencing.

He told me that about eight months earlier he lost control of his truck, which carried a full load of concrete, when the brakes failed while it was going down a hill. The truck wiped out several parked cars, scraped a stone fence and ended up on its side at the bottom of a ditch alongside the road. Somehow, Arnold was not badly injured, but as he lay in the hospital all he could think of was the terror he felt as the truck careened down the hill and the awful sounds of scraping metal and stone. By the time he recovered his physical health, he could no longer even think of driving a truck. In his mind, returning to his old job was not an option. The thought of driving a truck immobilized him with fear. He lived on disability income for awhile and over time he regressed to the point where he could not drive any vehicle, including his automobile. He had developed a true phobia and it was growing.

He said that at first he thought he could "tough it out" but he could not. He told me he was too embarrassed to admit his fears to anyone because they sounded so irrational, even to him. The phobia eventually generalized to the extent that if he even looked at a picture of a truck he broke out into a sweat and began trembling. In order to survive financially he could only take a job he could walk to. This low-paying job was along a ship channel and consisted of sitting in a lawn chair in the weeds in the hot summer sun with mosquitoes biting him while he recorded the registration numbers of boats passing by.

Finally his wife insisted that he see a professional so here he was. He did not think I could help him much, but it couldn't hurt much either.

One behavioral method for dealing with fears and phobias is to use an intervention called Systematic Desensitization. In a thorough intake interview the therapist ascertains the nature and scope of the fear, its context and the objective strength of the aversion to it. A hierarchical scale is constructed which ranks the varying levels of fear in relation to proximity and tolerance of the feared object or situation. Then the person is taught to relax by some method such as using calming imagery in combination with rhythmic breathing. When they have mastered this systematic relaxation and have achieved a comfortable state, they are introduced to thinking about the fear at the lowest level. When they can tolerate this, they are progressively introduced to the next level. If this elicits too strong an anxiety, they are returned to relaxation mode. By repeating this process over a long enough time span, first the lowest and then progressively the highest levels of anxiety are systematically eliminated. It is often very effective and commonly used in a variety of situations. I explained this to him and he agreed to try the therapy.

I first taught him to regulate his breathing and relax his muscles and then to use this systematic desensitization until he felt calm. He agreed that he would come in for a half hour each day. After we had practiced this technique in the office during several sessions, I asked his wife to help him practice at home as well. When he had mastered the method, I introduced him to some of the things that made him nervous step by step. It was a slow process, but he gradually overcame some of his symptoms. Eventually he was able to look at pictures of a car, then a truck, and then he could imagine seeing himself walk around them, sit in them, and think about maybe driving again. Slowly he progressed to the point where, with his wife's accompaniment and support, he was able to drive a car.

One day I told him I thought he was ready to go it on his own. He agreed and in the last session we just talked about ordinary things. I had a great deal of respect for his ability to confront and overcome his fears and I told him this. He seemed embarrassed. He never returned to his truck-driving job. The last time I saw him was by accident when I was shopping at a large building supply store; he was driving one of those electric powered forklifts around the aisles and refilling shelves. He seemed very happy and gave me a big smile, but it was clear he did not want to talk to me about it.

## C.   Welcome to the "Nam"

My work as a psychologist in the Veterans Administration provided ample exposure to veterans with Post Traumatic Stress Disorder (PTSD). In 1997 when I was an intern at the Houston VA Medical Center, the problem of PTSD was often still unrecognized or even denied as a valid diagnosis by clinicians. It was certainly less accepted than it is today. Later in my career I saw many veterans in my practice and provided consultation to an outpatient Vet Center. I was also in contact with the national outreach program and even gave seminars for them, but in the beginning I was still both learning myself and trying to educate others. When I gave public talks on PTSD and described some of the characteristics of the disorder, people would often come to me afterwards and relate their experiences with family or friends who had PTSD. For many this was the first time that they recognized the extent of or the reason for the emotions and behaviors they now recognized were caused by PTSD. As an example, one woman came up to me with tears in her eyes. She said her father was in WWII and never talked about his combat experiences. He was a loving parent and good provider, but he would periodically get raging drunk and punch holes in the walls. She now saw that he had suffered from PTSD all those years. He had died four years ago and she wished that she had known earlier that he had the problem and that there might have been help for him.

In these gatherings I would usually tell the story of a young Vietnam veteran I had seen in treatment. With the written permission of the veteran I would tell the story of his military experiences as a nineteen-year-old and play a brief recording in which he described some of them himself.

After basic training he was flown almost directly to Vietnam and within days of arrival he was sent to join his new unit. Nothing had prepared him for what he was about to experience. He, along with other green troops, was dropped by helicopter into a landing zone that was still "hot," meaning that it was still under potential attack by the enemy. He went with some other men of the unit to get water from a stream a short distance from their position. On the way back they were assaulted by hidden snipers and RPG (rifle propelled grenade) fire. He said that it was over in a minute and they had no chance to react or even to see where the enemy had gone. Several of the men were severely wounded and two were killed in the attack, but he was physically uninjured. As he watched, men he had just spoken to lay on the ground in agony or were being inserted into body bags. Helicopters quickly arrived and within moments carried the wounded and dead away. He stood shocked and confused. Eventually he went over to some other soldiers wanting to talk with them about the experience, but they just shrugged and said "Welcome to the Nam" and handed him a joint of marijuana. The rule seemed to be not to talk about it, not to dwell on it. This did not change for the thirteen months he was "in country."

I recalled seeing an automobile accident once where a car flipped over right in front of me and the driver was thrown out onto the pavement. I talked about this with everyone I knew for days before I got it out of my system and every time I got into my car I felt nervous that this might happen to me. My patient witnessed even more violent and personally threatening events and spent another year in harm's way. Even after he returned home "to the Land of the Big PX," he lived constantly with this first experience as well as many other traumas all stuffed inside him and etched in his memory forever.

I saw him on a regular basis over several months, but in the end, I do not think I helped this man very much. Perhaps I did not have the skills at the time to help him; perhaps he could never overcome the damage. I hope that was not the case. Perhaps telling his story will help others. I wish I could have done more for him.

## D.   Inner Adult to the Rescue

Not all PTSD casualties are directly related to combat. Even some military personnel in rear support units "cracked" from the stress of not knowing when they might be attacked or if the enemy would get through the fence some night and cut their throats. Others handled the bodies that stacked up waiting for shipment home. Still others survived, but felt enormous guilt and wondered why they lived while so many of their comrades died. One man never left the States but his job was to notify the families of those who had died and attend their funerals. When I saw him for therapy, each time he would cry about the grief of the families he had observed, and his own grief and guilt at having survived.

Another soldier I counseled had been a nineteen-year-old non-combatant cook. He was in what was considered a relatively secure rear position and thought he was safe, but as I understand it, there was no true non-combat zone in Vietnam. With no warning the entire area was attacked and overrun within minutes. He ran looking for whatever cover he could find. There was wild gunfire all around him and he dove into a shallow depression in the ground that offered some protection. There he waited with a cocked .45 caliber pistol and only a few rounds in the gun. He could hear shouts, running, and bullets fired all around him, but he was too afraid to move or join the battle. He expected any minute to see the enemy swarm over the top of the small mound of dirt that offered minimal cover. He said he shook so much that he did not think he could have even fired the gun if he was attacked. One of his thoughts was that it would be better to kill himself than be taken captive; another, that he was a coward because he did not leap up and engage the attackers. All of his fears concentrated when he heard the sound of soldiers approaching. To his great relief, what he heard was the American combat team that finally rescued him. Even though he never faced live fire again, the incident continued to haunt him.

Despite a successful civilian career and a good family life, he still never felt secure again and lived in almost constant fear of attack. At night he would compulsively check and re-check the locks on doors and windows and peer into the street to be sure that he and his family were safe. He periodically had terrifying dreams of being shot and experienced waking flashbacks. He often drank too much and he never watched war movies. He did not like any reminders of his time in the service.

After acquiring this history, I asked him if he would be willing to try an experiment even though as I warned him it might seem a little strange to him. I had read about and discussed with a few other therapists a technique that had at times been successful with other PTSD patients. I told him that this would be the first time I had tried this, but that I thought that in his case it might be useful. If he did not like it or it was not helping we could try something else. He agreed.

I had him close his eyes, relax and then conjure up an image of himself as he was today: strong and competent and, most of all, alive. I asked him to include the successes in his current life and to recall times when he had stood up for what he thought was right. We spent enough time on this exercise that he could envision himself completely and in the present. Then I had him go back in his imagination and find the young boy that was himself in Vietnam and remember how he felt then. I wanted him to understand that at that age being frightened was natural and acceptable. Despite being clearly uncomfortable with this he was able to do it. Then I put him in the role of his "adult self." Somewhat like a "guardian angel" he was to talk to and reassure the boy that he would survive and that he, the adult he grew into, would always be there by his side to help and protect him. He did this and said later that somehow it seemed natural to talk to himself in this way. He said that as both man and boy he utilized the knowledge and wisdom of his present circumstances and the confidence of both grew.

For several sessions we continued the different settings in which he had felt anxious in life and in between sessions he practiced similar scenarios at home. Finally he said he was ready to deal with the original trauma and we reserved the full hour for this. He was a little nervous at first, but as he talked through his experience of crouching in the ditch his voice grew steadier and in the end he clearly said, "It's alright now; I'm here with you." He opened his eyes and told me that it really was alright now and he could move on with his life. It was a dramatic moment for both of us.

At last he came in for a final appointment and said that in his imagination he had now stayed with the boy over time until he returned to the US and grew to his present age. He had completely united the images and he had no more need of his "guide" and by extension, with me. It was the last time I saw him.

We talk a lot now about connecting with the Inner Child; he was able to do so on a very deep level and he effectively nurtured that child with his Inner Adult. In essence I did not do the therapy, he did. I just directed it. I think that is what made him feel so proud and competent in the end. I was asked once why I did not suggest a faith to guide him. Many people might find this equally comforting. As I knew from the intake interview he was not religious.

As for me, I also looked for and found my Inner Adult and I provide him a bit of work to do from time to time in supporting my own needy Inner Child.

# E.  Unhappy Anniversary

Many people do not accept the concept of an unconscious, but I have seen too many examples of it in action to doubt there is one. If you have ever observed someone making a "Freudian Slip" or you have done something unexpected and later wondered why you ever could have done that, welcome to the club. Sometimes our dreams may provide a "Royal Road to the Unconscious" if we pay attention to them, but most of the time the unconscious operates beneath our level of awareness.

In addition to everyday experience there is excellent academic research to support its presence. One interesting example of the unconscious on our lives is the phenomena of an Anniversary Reaction. This is when you may feel grief and sadness on the anniversary of the death of someone close to you even if you are unaware that this day is the specific date of the occurrence. The brain even seems to maintain its own calendar. A personal example of this occurred after my father died. Even today I cannot remember the date of his death, but several years ago I was experiencing a very rough day with no apparent reason. I was depressed, grouchy and distracted. Unbeknown to me my wife told our children to leave me alone and explained to them that my mood was caused by the three-year anniversary of my father's death and I was sad. I had no conscious idea that this was the exact date, but I clearly was mourning him. Only when my sons gathered around me in concern and told me what their mother had said did I realize the truth of this. I even had to look at the calendar to verify that this was the exact date. Then I let myself experience how much I missed my father and I came into conscious touch with the deep loss I felt and with my sorrow. Afterward it was as if a burden was lifted from me.

Even though I knew about the anniversary reaction and had experienced it myself, I was surprised when I again encountered it in one of my patients. George was a referral with severe anxiety. He was retired from the steel industry and was a widower who lived alone. He had come into the clinic that day saying that he "just couldn't take it anymore." He repeated this to me during our initial meeting. When I asked him to tell me more about this, he said that the strangest thing was that it didn't happen all the time but came and went. Sometimes weeks went by without a problem. Further exploration revealed that about a year-and-a- half ago two men who broke into his house because they thought he had drugs and money hidden inside of it terrorized him. He did not have any dope and he supposed that the men had mistaken his address for the one next door where a neighbor did deal drugs. He told them this, but they refused to believe him.

After tearing apart much of his house while they searched but did not finding any drugs or money, they pushed him into his bedroom and angrily threatened to kill him if he did not tell them where he had hidden his stash. As you can imagine he was in great fear for his life and the two intruders just seemed to be getting angrier at not finding anything. He was pushed to the floor and was lying there with one man standing over him. This man said that he was going to count to ten and if George did not tell them the truth he would pull the trigger and blow his brains out. George was sure he was going to die, but then for a moment he overcame his terror and remembered that his own gun, a revolver, was under the nearby bed. He reached out his arm, found the weapon, pulled it out and at about the eighth count shot the gunman in the face. Before the man's partner could overcome his shock and respond to this unexpected turn of events, George was able to quickly turn his gun on him and shoot him as well. All six shots were fired. He had killed both attackers, but following a police investigation, he was eventually cleared of any wrongdoing.

From this history it will already seem clear to the reader where the source of the anxiety might have originated. This was reinforced when I asked him when his symptoms were at their worst. You do not often get an "aha!" response from patients, but this time the light suddenly dawned on him. He identified the period when he experienced severe panic attacks as being around the third Thursday of each month. This corresponded to the exact date of the attack and shooting. With this information he further pinpointed the worst time as being at about three in the afternoon, which was the exact time when the attack occurred. He said that he had never connected the two events before. It was especially interesting in that he sought therapy and was now seeing me only three days prior to this anniversary. His unconscious seemed to be speaking to him at some level.

The realization that in all probability this was the origin of his anxiety and the fact that he was able to see this clearly and talk about it was important. In many ways he had already begun the healing process and we had begun work on emotional catharsis. Of course I made an immediate appointment for him on Thursday. On the "fatal" day he came to my office early in the afternoon and we spent three hours together revisiting the event over and over and desensitizing him to the memories. He had never told the story to anyone except during the police investigation. Each time he told it to me he was noticeably calmer and I would reassure him that he was gaining more control over his anxieties. Three o'clock passed without conscious awareness on his part. By four he had begun to drift from the event and was sharing a few other details of his life with me.

For the next several months on the Thursday of the shooting he spent at least an hour with me. Eventually he did not show for an appointment and when I called him, he said he no longer needed a "babysitter." He was over it.

An interesting sidelight is that over time what was also resolved in this process was his guilt over taking two lives. Logically he said he knew that the men had left him no choice, but it still weighed heavily upon his conscience. He said he could still see their faces sometimes and he wondered if they ever believed him about the drugs and if they really would have killed him. The police told him that they were certain the intruders would have killed him. The police investigation cleared him long ago, but he had not so easily forgiven himself. I think that in time the anxiety and the guilt both finally vanished together.

# F.   Blushing

Rosa (which is as clever as I will get with pseudonyms) told me that she came to me in desperation after she had "tried everything else." Her friends told her that maybe she should see a shrink. "So," she said anxiously, "here I am."

She had light-brown hair pulled back in a rather severe bun, wore a neatly tailored business suit, and exhibited a professional and straightforward manner as typified in her opening statement. She explained that she had a college degree in management and over several years had worked her way up from an entry-level clerical job to a mid-level position in management. Now at age thirty-two she encountered a problem that she defined as potentially career limiting. It was blushing.

She had a very pale skin color and from childhood on had blushed easily and often to the extent of turning bright red. This was accompanied by the feeling that her whole body was overheating. This characteristic was somewhat of a mild source of amusement among her friends. Her co-workers joked about it when she was at a lower pay grade, but presently she believed that it threatened her career. Now that she had moved up the corporate ladder she encountered more competition among others at her level, each of whom had their eyes on the next pay raise and promotion. It had become commonplace for her male counterparts to tease her or to elicit her blushing in other ways, particularly when they were in meetings at which the manager was present and they wanted to minimize her proposals. She believed that her co-workers intentionally triggered her blushing response at these times, especially if

30

a minor conflict existed between them or they wanted to make her look bad in front of her boss.

Increasingly she dreaded attendance at these meetings. Even worse, she supervised the work of four people and had come to realize that sometimes they used the fact of her easy blushing to undermine her authority. If she blushed when she was giving them directions or reprimanding them, the subordinates found it difficult to take her seriously and at times ignored her instructions or continued unacceptable behaviors. She was sure that they laughed at her frustration and perhaps even mocked her behind her back. It had reached the point where even anticipation of a conflict or any emotionally-laden experience would evoke a blush. She was thinking of quitting her job. She blushed heavily as she explained her problem to me.

Could I help her? First I explained that in general a person cannot voluntarily elicit responses such as blushing because they are controlled by the sympathetic nervous system. For example, you cannot voluntarily speed up or slow down your heart rate, raise or lower your temperature. You cannot blush intentionally even if you want to do so. (I encourage you to try this at home.) Based on this neurological constraint, I suggested that the solution to her problem might be that she try to initiate a blush or intensify it rather than fight it. This is a technique based on Paradoxical Intervention formulated by Viktor Frankl in his book *Man's Search for Meaning*[2]. It has many applications; you will read about another one in the next case history.

I told her that as an initial step I would ask her to blush on command. First as a demonstration I would blush. I

---

[2] Victor Frankl, *Man's Search for Meaning* (Boston: Beacon Press, 1959).

would shut my eyes and think of one of my most embarrassing moments. Nothing happened. Next I puffed out my cheeks and blew air trying to turn red. Soon we were both laughing. Now it was her turn to practice. With her eyes shut she imagined a recent event in the office where she blushed so severely that she considered running from her office and hiding. After a minute or two her visage remained reasonably pale. However, this was just imagination, she protested, what about real life? Suddenly I leaned forward and snapped: "Don't tell me my business, you're just not trying hard enough." She sat back shocked at my change of demeanor and was clearly both angry and confused. "I am," she responded just as forcefully. I sat back smiling "Yes, but you are not blushing even now, are you?" She was not, even with the strong stimulus of emotional confrontation I had provided.

By the end of the hour, she was doing quite well at not blushing no matter how hard she tried. We role-played several situations that had proved difficult for her in the past and she did not blush. Then I again tried to trick her by asking mildly uncomfortable questions such as did she have a boy friend and what did they like to do together, but she still did not blush. When our time was up, I encouraged her to continue this practice frequently and I would see her again in a week. Meanwhile, in order to increase her control, she was to challenge her friends and family to make her blush if they could and she was to intentionally put herself in situations that had been difficult in the past. Whenever possible, she was to prepare herself by trying to blush as hard as she could before each encounter. I do not think she was totally convinced it would work but, as she said, she had tried everything else so why not this too?

At her next appointment I observed a difference in her demeanor when she walked into the office and sat down.

She seemed much more self-assured and less reserved. She was smiling like she couldn't wait to tell me the news. She laughingly told me that she had driven everyone nearly crazy by challenging them to try to make her blush and that eventually they all gave up. She became, in her words, practically "blush proof."

She reported that her blushing was not totally cured, but it was much less a problem for her at work. At times when she was caught off guard, she would feel her face getting warm, and then she would tell herself not to give into it, but to even try harder, and show everyone what a real blush looked like. She took special pride that the first time one of the male employees who had been one of her worst antagonists intentionally tried to rattle her, she was instead able to turn the tables on him so successfully that she made him blush. I did not ask her for details on what she did, but she said that everyone laughed at him and the harassment decreased from then on. For better or for worse, she was now more accepted as "one of the guys." She had confidence that by using her new technique she could continue to improve on controlling her blushing.

We talked a little more, but it was clear that at this time she neither wanted nor required further intervention. I left it to her to decide whether she would make another appointment if she ever needed one, but I never heard from her again. In the future I was able to use this technique in several other cases of blushing or in similar problems of discomfort in social situations. It was frequently, but not always, effective although it seldom occurred with such rapidity as in Rosa's case.

Note: I suppose I should be the one blushing here for my bragging. I specifically included this case because it is very similar to one I published earlier in the journal, *Psychotherapy: Theory, Research and Practice.*[3] That article has been cited a few times and I am proud to say is referenced in the book that I mentioned above by Viktor Frankl.

---

[3] J. Alexander Boeringa, "Blushing: A Modified Behavioral Intervention Using Paradoxical Intention." ***Psychotherapy: Theory, Research and Practice*** 20, no. 4, (1983): 441-444.

## G.    The Hallway Walker

In one of the hospitals where I worked there was a long hallway coming from the back parking lots. If I arrived too late to find closer parking in front or if it was raining and I wanted cover for the walk to my office, I sometimes used this hallway. Going this way I would pass the geriatric unit that housed many of the oldest and sickest patients. After a time I began to recognize a few of the patients and particularly one old man. Each time I saw him he was in the hallway in his pajamas holding on to the railing along the wall and he seemed to be waiting until I passed. When I said hello, he would look up but never returned the greeting. I eventually wondered what he was doing there and so I unobtrusively paused at the end of the hall to watch him. Step by struggling step he slowly moved along the hall while tightly gripping the rail and shuffling one foot in front of the other. I tried to imagine where he was going that was so important. The trip seemed to cost him so much effort, especially when he could have easily used a wheelchair or gotten a staff member to help him. Again, hidden from his view I watched. At the end of the hall he would pause for a long time as if building up strength or courage, or both, and then propel himself across the four foot gap to the safety of the opposite rail. Once there he would as slowly walk to the other end of the hall where almost twenty minutes later he would repeat the leap to the other side and return.

I asked the nursing staff about him and they confirmed that he did this each day for at least an hour before returning to his room and lying in his bed for a while clearly exhausted. They said that he did not ask for or seem to want help. In fact, when they offered, he refused it. They thought that it was his way of maintaining his independence; I did too. Being a nosey psychologist, of course I wanted to talk to him and find out more about him and his story, but I did not attempt to interfere; I think it would have been viewed as an insult.

I have tremendous respect for this man. To me he was as much a hero as any soldier bravely confronting an enemy or an athlete training for the Olympics. His leap of faith from one side of the hallway to the other reminded me of when I was a youth. There were cliffs overlooking a lake where we used to go swimming and it was considered the height of daring-do to jump or dive from the highest cliff into the water far below. In a way it was a rite of passage for those who swam there and if you did not do so at least once you were never properly admitted into the inner circle of the group. At times, the new inductee would stand there at the edge for hours working up his nerve. Some boys finally jumped and rose from the water whooping with exhilaration. Some finally turned back and left for home never to swim there again. I won't tell you which group I belonged to.

His determination in the face of the potentially debilitating injury he might have sustained if he had fallen took a great deal of nerve on his part. There was no club to join, no gang of supporters urging him on or congratulating him when he made the leap. Each day he faced the challenge by himself, on his own terms, and a result of his own decision. I could not help but wonder if I in his circumstances would do as well. I am only sorry that I did not make more of an effort to befriend him and learn more about him. Selfishly, I think that perhaps I also wanted to know how he had built and maintained the tremendous will and reserves of courage that he exhibited. I might need a similar strength someday.

## H.    The Hypnotic Doctor B?

This title is the very kind inscription written by my friend Deirdre Barrett for me on the front page of her book on hypnosis.[4] It is especially flattering because she is a much more accomplished hypnotist than I. I confess that I really do not know how hypnosis works and despite attending seminars and training courses with some of the leading exponents in the field, I am still not sure that anyone does. However, I have seen it work and be surprisingly powerful at times. I suspect that at least some patients respond especially well to what might be the mystic quality of it, and for others, I do not know. I do know that when I have used hypnosis it was often successful in achieving the desired results. I am left with the explanation that it is a combination of deep relaxation, intense concentration and a willingness to accept suggestion. If people want to change, they will find a way to do so that works for them.

Most of the public's perception about hypnosis comes from books, movies and stage shows designed to entertain. I derived my own first impressions from the backs of comic books. Here lurid illustrations depicted scantily dressed young women under the control of some Svengali-like character with rays shooting out of his eyes. Only in my dreams. What you see in the hypnotism act of The Great Whomever primarily depends on audience members who want to show off for a while. There is nothing done on stage that cannot be repeated by anyone who is willing to go along with the gag. In addition, no one can be made to do under

---

[4] Deirdre Barrett, PhD, *The Pregnant Man and Other Cases from a Hypnotherapist's Couch* (New York: Random House, 1998).

"hypnosis" something they do not want to do. Having said this, people will follow suggestions that are in their best interests to accept, like quitting smoking. It works if you want it to. The following are some examples.

When I was on the faculty at the Medical School in Galveston, I worked on a mental health referral service that primarily answered consults from physicians requesting either further diagnosis or adjunct psychological treatments for their patients. A group of medical students was assigned to me on a part-time basis and I held rounds with them. First we met in a conference room and they would present the cases assigned to them. They reported the history and progress of a patient and they offered their own psychiatric diagnoses and suggested interventions. We then discussed the cases as a group and I would give my initial impressions, offer theoretical formulations and make further assignments. Following this, we would all go to see patients who promised to be the best teaching cases with all of us sweeping down the halls in our varied lengths of white coats and me leading the charge. It was heady stuff for a psychologist! We would descend upon and surround the bed of some poor soul who could not escape. In practice, I always knocked first and asked permission of the patient to interview them. I thought this propriety was only common courtesy although I noticed that it was not always followed in hospitals I worked in. I hoped that I was then about to teach the students by example what to do.

One patient who tolerated our invasion was referred because he had serious medical concerns and constant anxiety over his condition. I could do nothing to improve his prognosis but after a few moments of conversation it became clear that he needed some help in "chilling out." I suggested the use of hypnosis to him and he agreed.

In addition to encouraging deep relaxation with him as part of the induction, I encouraged him to concentrate on my voice. I then used a progression of guided images to assist him to enter a somewhat altered state: a place in which he might be unusually receptive to my suggestions.

After asking him to un-tense his muscles and slow his breathing, I asked him to imagine in some detail a bright sunny day with him looking out over the blue waters of a lake and wispy white clouds floating overhead. I asked him to tell me when he relaxed and could see this clearly in his imagination. I introduced a few other details and suggested a small island to which he could return when he wanted to re-experience the pleasant state he was in now. All was going well until I asked if he could see the distant shore of this island. He said no. That concerned me so I asked why and he replied that a large sailboat was momentarily blocking his vision.

The degree of intensity and depth of the state he had entered to be able to add such solid and self-generated elements to the experience surprised me. It was unusual especially for the first session. I think that the possibility of finding some escape from his anxiety was very strong and he took the first opportunity offered him.

I could see a little bit of wonder on the faces of the students and a slight respect for my ability that is generally rare and difficult to get from young doctors. Alternatively, perhaps this was this just my own fantasy. After a moment he said that, OK, the boat had now passed and he could see the shore and an awaiting pier. I added a few other potentially helpful elements to the scene and told him that the next time he would enter into hypnosis even more easily. I left him with the thought that he could also utilize the relaxation and visualization technique on his own. I then asked him to gradually "wake up" as I counted from five backwards to one.

On leaving the room, one student asked if I had previously seen the patient and bribed him to fake the sailboat bit for my demonstration. That pleased me a great deal. At least one student had been impressed enough to arouse his skepticism. That is always a good sign.

# I.    Other Examples

I team taught interview techniques with Dr. Sharma, a physician whose specialty was in obstetrics. She was always a delight to work with because she had the credentials and hospital-wide reputation that impressed the third year medical students. I could speak about helping patients become comfortable and the nuances of drawing information from them. As I will mention again, patients do not always provide all of the details needed to make a diagnoses or help them. They frequently leave out details. In this case a pregnant woman could not take the usual anesthetics or medications because of a complicating medical condition. The problem was that Lupe did not have any previous medical records and only "mentioned" the detail concerning anesthetics to her physician in her sixth month of pregnancy. Dr. Sharma specialized in high-risk pregnancies so the woman was referred to her. Dr. Sharma asked me if I would hypnotize the patient and be present at the birth to ease any pain problems. Lupe was willing to try this.

In our practice session together, Lupe easily reached a semi-trance state and felt confident that she could go through the birthing with hypnosis alone. She was an excellent subject with a strong will. When I first interviewed Lupe and her husband, he seemed supportive and I soon realized that it would be more appropriate for him to be her guide instead of me. After that I included them both in the process and essentially taught him to do relaxation and suggestion with her; in other words, hypnosis. The couple continued to practice together with my guidance, and Dr. Sharma came in once to share with them the routine of the delivery room and satisfy herself that they were ready to have the baby this way. They were doing so well that I saw no need to be present at the birth and they agreed. I would have liked to since it would be the first time I had used hypnosis in such a situation, but it was clearly their time to be together and share a close bonding experience. I would only have interfered in the process. I only asked for a follow-up after the baby was born.

According to everyone involved, the outcome was both satisfactory and very successful. Lupe delivered with a minimum of what we men like to call "discomfort." The hypnosis was a good adjunct to the standard Lamaze techniques taught in the class the couple had taken. In addition, Dr. Sharma was especially pleased with the decision for Lupe's husband to be the one who was able to be not only present, but so helpful in the process.

I mentioned using hypnoses to help people quit smoking and I have used it a few times to assist people trying to kick this and other habits. My first case was a man who was extremely susceptible to hypnoses, in fact so much so that I thought he was faking a "trance" to make me feel better. With this in mind, I asked him if I might videotape our sessions to which he readily agreed and signed the necessary paperwork. He was making excellent progress and I wanted to try post-hypnotic suggestion in which a direction is given under hypnosis although it is forgotten to the conscious mind but then carried out when the subject is later "awakened." In this case, I told him that since he "no longer smoked," he would be unable to light a cigarette, and that he would later forget that I had told him this.

After the session I asked if he would like a cigarette and he said yes, he was down to two a day and one would taste good right now. When he attempted to light it though, either the match would go out or he could not get it anywhere near the cigarette. After several attempts he seemed genuinely mystified as to why he could not light the cigarette and he gave several explanations such as being nervous or the matches being of inferior quality. When I showed him the tape and the post-hypnotic suggestion, he refused to believe this could have had an effect. He accused me of playing a trick on him. Eventually I re-hypnotized him and told him that now he could again light the cigarette, which he later did. He needed to quit smoking, not believe in hypnotism.

I kept this tape for many years and showed it to other professionals who agreed that it did indeed appear to be a genuine case of post-hypnotic suggestion. I am only sorry that over the years I lost this tape in one of my many moves. The man went on to attend several other sessions and eventually quit smoking entirely. As far as the efficacy of hypnosis (or whatever we chose to call it) I also have the testimony of my own brother-in-law who over the years tried many methods and was finally able to stop smoking with the aid of hypnotic therapy. As I said earlier on, I do believe it can work if you want it to work. As to how it works, I remain skeptical, but I have seen how useful it can be.

# IV.  DIFFERENT STROKES

Working in a hospital I of course encountered more people with physical illnesses and problems related to them than I ever did in private practice. Sometimes when physicians were frustrated by unresponsive or troublesome patients, they would do a quick referral to another department. In polite language this is called "Buffing and Turfing" and it is a technique I first read about in the book "The House of God" by Dr. Samuel Shem. As an example, a busy emergency room physician might shift a psychiatric patient to a "shrink" if possible and thereby reduce his or her own workload. Or perhaps a psychiatrist would find a slight medical condition in a new patient and refer to a medical service. The patient might eventually return, but by then someone else would probably be on duty or at least the patient would be off your hands for a while. Of course in less polite language this ploy is more often referred to as "dumping."

Since it is unusual to find a medical problem unaccompanied by a psychological response to it, mental health services were especially vulnerable to turfing consults. This was especially so if it looked like a patient was going to be difficult to deal with, such as exhibiting excessive sadness, anger or other "messy" emotions. Of course, if a patient had unusual symptoms that did not easily fit common medical diagnoses, it might well be true that the symptom had an underlying emotional origin. I welcomed the chance to work with these patients because I always thought that I had something useful to offer. In addition, they frequently were especially interesting. These cases could fill a book by themselves, but here are four examples: Shirley, Rhona, John and Mrs. Pluedine.

# A. A Needle Phobic

A physician in the hospital where I worked called me and asked if I would come to meet a patient she thought might benefit from my help. I am generally suspicious of these "on the spot" consults, especially since I was not given further details. This could mean that it was an attempt to get rid of a difficult patient by transferring them to another care provider, the process known as "turfing." In my experience, many medical people do not like to admit that they have not succeeded in diagnosing or treating a patient and that they are stumped enough to seek psychological assistance. In this case it helped that this doctor and I had worked together quite well with other patients. She appreciated the help I provided her patients in the past and I always sought her out if I thought a patient of mine might be experiencing an undiagnosed medical problem.

When I arrived at her office, the physician introduced me to Shirley, gave me her medical history, and explained how she thought I might help. Shirley listened carefully, asked a few questions, and seemed agreeable to my suggestions. She was a husky and quite muscular young woman who was married and held a responsible job in the community. Recently diagnosed with diabetes, she needed periodic injections of insulin. The problem was that due to a childhood illness that required frequent blood drawing, she was terrified of needles. She refused the shots from the nurse and she could not imagine having her husband give them to her or ever being able to give them to herself. Alternate methods, such as diet, exercise and oral medications, failed to control her symptoms. Without the injections she could become seriously ill or die. She had allowed the doctor to give her one injection, but was now refusing to accept any more even though the necessity of doing so and the possible consequences were clearly explained to her.

Further attempts to give her the insulin ranged from trying to talk her into it, to threats of what might happen if she did not have them, to giving her a light tranquilizer when she needed an injection. Clearly this could not be done each time and none of her caregivers were willing to contemplate doing so. For one thing she could not come into the hospital each time and she might find herself in a medical emergency where she could not wait.

Unfortunately, right in the middle of these discussions she had an unrelated injury in which emergency room care providers had to hold her down to start an IV. In the course of her struggles, a needle broke and it needed to be dug out from her arm. To complete the necessary procedures they had to use leather restraints and a general anesthetic. Needless to say, this did not help alleviate her fears.

Shirley was a reasonably intelligent person who knew that she needed treatment, but she was terrified at the thought of an injection. I considered using relaxation techniques and systematic desensitization, but we did not have the time for her to become proficient in this and she needed at least daily injections. Hypnosis was another option, but she remained too tense to begin an induction. I decided to try a form of in vivo desensitization by gradually moving towards the goal by practicing incremental steps in the process. I was determined that I would be able to help her somehow. For one thing this was an interesting case for me and I pride myself at being good at problem solving. And to be completely honest maybe my ego wanted to succeed to show medicine that I could do it?

I spent a good deal of time with her in which we addressed all of her fears including the fact that over time she would have to learn to tolerate different injection sites. We compared this challenge to others she had faced in her life and I asked her to bring the same dedication and focus to the task she displayed in lifting weights.

The first step was for her to sit in a treatment room until she felt calm. Then I showed her syringes, medicine bottles and the other paraphernalia required until she became accustomed to being able to look at them. I asked a nurse to show her all of the steps in preparation for an injection. With Shirley's permission the nurse would then swab her and eventually mimic a shot by pinching her. To say that she was totally calm during all of this would be an outright lie, but she did tolerate it.

Next, she began to consider a theoretical time when she might consider the receiving the shots and she practiced this in her imagination. Finally because she knew that she needed to do this, she progressed to the point where she was ready to try to face the injection cold without drugs or restraints. I went to support her on the big day. She spent fifteen minutes getting relaxed and preparing for the insulin shot, but in the end she could not go through with it. Once more she was given a sedative in order to receive the insulin.

My schedule did not permit me to be with her each time she needed insulin and the next day I had a full schedule and could not be with her. At about four o'clock I received a phone call from Shirley, who wanted me to know that she had received her injection without outside assistance and she thought she could continue to do so. She said, "After all, it's really no big deal is it?" Ouch!

For her success she received a great deal of enthusiastic reinforcement from the staff and when I saw her the following day I added my own congratulations. In terms of the original goal, the treatment was not a total success because she was never able to administer her own insulin, but she did make significant progress. I received reports a few weeks later that she was allowing her husband or another family member to give the injections to her.

Courage comes in all flavors. I admire Shirley in that she was able to confront a fear as great and deeply rooted as hers. Does anyone really like shots?

# B.  Rhona

Patients do not usually mind being shifted if is to a specialist. They appreciate that their complex problem is receiving special attention. Being sent to a mental health discipline, however, has quite a different impact. They feel, sometimes legitimately, that the referring doctor considers their problems to be "all in their head." This implies to them that they are being treated as a "nut case" and in some cases they may be correct. This can obviously create a hostile beginning for the "shrink" who sees them. It is the first thing to deal with and I always begin by acknowledging that they might have this impression, but I assure them that I do not see them that way and that their problems will be taken seriously. Taking the time to listen to them first goes a long way in achieving their trust and acceptance. It indicates to them that I accept the reality of their concerns and it serves to "legitimize" them before I begin discussing any possible interventions.

When she was referred to me by her primary physician, Rhona felt like she was being treated not only as a hypochondriac, but even more unfairly as a drug seeker and abuser. She was a twenty-eight-year-old woman with a long history of severe migraine headaches. There was a great deal of concern by her physician that she might be overusing the medications he was prescribing for her, either addicted to them or "diverting" them to be sold as street drugs. In addition there had been several complaints from the emergency room that she was showing up too often and the same concerns about her obtaining narcotic medications.

Unless persuaded otherwise, I usually begin therapy with a patient as they present themselves. There may be other complications or contributing causes for their problems, but I believe you have to start where they tell you they are. For this reason I focused on her migraines and, as she complained, asked her the same questions she had already answered "a million times." The only difference being that I concentrated more on the stressors in her life.

I had already read her treatment history and there was no indication of recreational or other illegal drug use anywhere in her past. Since it was clearly such a hot topic, I largely ignored drug taking and only asked her about the usual over-the-counter alcohol and tobacco usage. Since stress is clearly a possible trigger for migraines, I focused on the sources of stress in her life. There were several, including a job she hated and an ugly divorce initiated by her husband who was now dating her ex-best friend. That would be a full load for anyone. As we began to talk about these things, I tried to reduce some of her worst tensions and teach her to relax.

A few weeks after beginning therapy with Rhona, I was informed that she had been hospitalized. I went to see her as soon as I was able to do so. I did not recognize her because her face was contorted with pain. Only by reading the nametag at the end of the bed did I know it was her. To use the vernacular, she looked like death warmed over. Slowly she pieced together the circumstances that sent her to the hospital.

She experienced the unmistakable signs, or prodrome, of the onset of a migraine so she went to the emergency room because her physician did not have clinic hours on the weekend and her regular medications were not controlling the pain. Even though there were not many patients in the waiting room, she had been made to wait for hours and was largely ignored by the staff. When she finally asked when she would be seen, she was treated rudely as if she were a dope-seeking junky. After two hours, she felt her migraine worsening and in frustration left without being seen. By that evening her condition had deteriorated to the point that she had a friend drive her back to the emergency room. After one look at her and a check of her vital signs, she was quickly admitted.

I met with the primary physician who had referred her and he agreed that obviously the migraines were not under control and they were worse than he had first imagined. He agreed to try a more aggressive protocol with her. When she needed refills for medications, they would be provided up to a defined dosage and frequency without question. He would see her on a more frequent basis but, as a precaution, if she ever exceeded the prescribed limits, she would need his approval before a prescription was renewed. If she showed up in the ER, he would be called to determine what was to be done, but in any case, she would be seen with, as he put it, "a little greater expediency." For my part, when Rhona was discharged from the hospital, I would increase our sessions to twice a week. I did so and she was diligent about keeping the appointments and making the health changes recommended by her entire medical team.

No miracles occurred. Neither the medications nor I cured her migraines, but they did occur less frequently and with less intensity. As importantly, there was medical relief available to her when she most needed it. When I last saw her, she was controlling her diet and was significantly reducing her stress levels on her own. She found a new job, was divorced and had a new boyfriend. Maybe these changes worked more magic than I or the meds did. Who knows? I have my own guesses.

This is a case in which psychotherapy had negligible success, but on the strength of my standing as a professional, I was able to broker a compromise that helped my patient in a way that she had not been able to negotiate by herself. Sometimes you have to get out of the office to effect the change that most needs to occur in the patient's life. There have been other cases where my main contribution has been to assist in adjusting not a patient's psyche but their circumstances. I do not feel bad about this. Any wisdom I have gained over the years may be in first recognizing the limits of my skills. Most of the circumstances in a patient's life are far beyond my awareness or my control.

## C.  John

---

John was a twenty-two-year-old man who came to me because his multidisciplinary treatment team suggested to him I would be a good person to talk to and that I might be able to help him with a problem he was experiencing. I have found in my practice that physicians are often incredible in what they do. They can literally dig down into a person's insides and fix things that I never want to see. However, when it comes to the human emotions accompanying physical problems, physicians are sometimes at a loss. This is not true of all physicians of course. Many of them are among the most caring people on the planet, but some of them feel more comfortable when they hide behind their stethoscopes and scrubs. In John's case, the doctors performed brilliantly in rearranging body parts, but were embarrassed when confronted with a whole person. That they passed to the behavioral medicine team which, in this case, happened to be me.

John had a condition that required him to wear a colostomy bag, probably for the rest of his life. He had adjusted well to living with it himself, but now he was confronted with decisions that would affect his social life. Of immediate concern was the question of whether to tell or not tell his friends about his colostomy.

When I met John, I was impressed with his overall cheerful attitude and generally upbeat personality. I immediately liked him and I could not help but wonder how I might respond if I was in his situation. He stated that in spite of his past medical difficulties and his present situation his approach was knowledgeable, direct and unembarrassed when discussing anything. This was a problem to be solved not a tragedy to be obsessed over.

54

He was a good looking man with all of the interests and urges of his age group. Due to the demands of his medical treatments and frequent hospitalizations, he had had only one girlfriend in his life and she had "moved on." He somewhat shyly said that although there had been a lot of heavy petting early on, they had never arrived at what he termed "the moment of truth."

Now with his medical condition fairly stabilized he was ready to "take it to the next level." The big problem was how to approach the issue of "the bag" when he began a relationship with a woman, especially the timing. It was not something he wanted to introduce too early: "Hi, I'm John. I'm a Leo with Scorpio rising and I wear a colostomy bag." On the other hand, there clearly needed to be some discussion prior to any of the intimacies that he hoped would occur in his life. I truthfully told him that I had never encountered a similar situation and I did not have any standard answer to his questions in my repertoire. What I suggested was that we explore possibilities that he might feel comfortable with and then he would decide what seemed to work best for him.

After much discussion his decision was first to inform and educate his closest friends. He would check out their reactions and then ask them for both suggestions and support. Next he planned to leak the information (pun clearly intended!) to allow it to become general knowledge among some of his other acquaintances. This way the word would be spread and the potential impact somewhat defused.

In subsequent visits he reported that all in all his buddies took it pretty well and, as is the nature of men in this age group, after a short time they found ways to poke fun of him in the same spirit as they did with everyone and everything else. There is nothing like a good laugh to ease any tensions and, as demonstrated above, he already had a good sense of humor.

The second stage of the plan also worked reasonably well and, after an initial buzz within the larger group, interest quickly died down. As far as he could tell, knowledge of the colostomy bag became commonplace and accepted. His female friends did not consider the bag to be an impediment to intimacy as long as preparations were made in advance, such as temporarily removing the bag and assuring the partner there would be nothing "gross." His only comment regarding the sexual aspect of his dating was that it was "much improved."

In this case there was little I provided that was technically therapy in the traditional sense. I offered encouragement and the opportunity for him to bounce ideas off a neutral professional. You could say I was a "Dutch Uncle" of sorts, which is appropriate I guess given my background of having each of my grandparents having been born in the Netherlands. I certainly admired his courage and respected his inner strength and honesty. I also wonder how well I would have dealt with the same circumstances. It put a few of my own problems in perspective. By now he might be a father with children the age he was when he came to see me. I hope so.

# D.  Mrs. Pluedine

Mrs. Pluedine, a late-middle-aged woman, was admitted to a medical ward with "complete paralysis to her lower extremities in the absence of positive neurological findings." The medical consensus was that this was a case of outright faking or, more kindly, conversion hysteria. When she did not improve in spite of every test and intervention the practitioners could think of other than surgery, they referred her to me for a consultation. This may have been a casebook example of turfing, but I was delighted to see it. I do not like referrals that include a treatment plan, such as "Please do psychological testing." Instead, I prefer to be told the problem and, as an independent professional and specialist, I will decide how best to answer the needs of the patient. In this case, the staff wanted me to "do hypnosis" and in essence relocate her from their unit where she took up space, absorbed resources, and made them feel ineffectual. I suspected that some of the staff also would have liked me to fail miserably and thereby reinforce their perception of the mental health profession.

When I met Mrs. Pluedine, I was straightforward in telling her that I was a psychologist and I was seeing her because of her current problem. She knew that meant "shrink," but she accepted me graciously anyway. I did not focus on her ailment, but talked with her for an hour-and-a-half about her life. She told me about her impoverished childhood, a traumatic rape at an early age, raising seven children, and a husband who was a "good man" but not especially attentive to her. The fact was that the only time he had ever brought her flowers or showed much concern for her was during this hospital stay. They lived in an area known for abject poverty, inferior education, and deep-rooted suspicion of the outside world, including anyone who wore a suit, and especially doctors and shrinks. She was surprised when I told her I would visit with her again and left without "doing anything."

In retrospect, her problem seems simple and I believe I am correct in my formulation of its origin and progress. In her unsophisticated way and totally without conscious volition, I think that not too different from a person contemplating suicide, she had decided that life had disappointed her and left her boxed into a corner from which there was no escape. This was the only way she would ever get a rest and have her long ignored needs met. Her unconscious had formulated a plan and her body unwittingly complied.

It was a case of her body "acting out" what her mind did not dare to say. I would definitely not use hypnosis. As an unsophisticated subject she would probably respond rapidly, but that would be tricking her and I wanted her to make a conscious decision. To employ an overused term, I hoped to empower her. In addition, I suspected that the early inability to resist her rapes left her feeling both used and powerless. Her entire life had been an inevitable progression of meeting the needs of men. These demands began in childhood and continued on from her husband to her children and probably now her grandchildren.

The last thing she needed was for yet another male to coerce her to do something she might not want to do. Instead, I reinforced the legitimacy of her emotional needs and I suggested other ways she might satisfy them. Her slight smiles and gradual improvement indicated she understood and could make small changes but was still somewhat constrained by the expectations of her culture.

I also met with Mr. Pluedine when he was able to take off from work to make the one-hundred mile trip from where the family lived in a backwoods rural area. He was as trapped as she was in the culture in which they had lived all of their lives. He was, I believe, a genuinely good man who sincerely loved his wife and as he said to me at one point, he "would have given his own life for her recovery." I strongly impressed upon him that too much hard work and stress might cause her condition to return once she was cured and had returned home. It was up to him to help and protect her from overexertion. She needed his support and occasional reminders of the love he had shown during her hospitalization. He agreed and said he would see to it that the rest of the family did not put too much of a burden on her either. I asked if he could he imagine her as the young girl he had courted and he said that yes, he could see that and it brought back fond memories. I noticed soon after that there were fresh flowers in her room after each of his visits.

It was about this time that she told her doctors that little by little she could feel the strength returning to her legs, then she was able to move them a little, and later she was shuffling down the hallway with her solicitous husband holding her by the waist. She recovered slowly, but perhaps not fast enough for the ward staff. When Mrs. Pluedine was discharged, I watched the woman who had entered the hospital in a wheel chair walk from the front door to the awaiting car by herself.

I especially would have liked to follow up on her to see if the gains she made persisted, not only the physical ones but also the larger changes in her life that, if my theory is correct, her body had fought for her to obtain. Those were a small increase in personal freedom, and increased respect. I hoped so. I admired the cleverness of her unconscious and the naïve ingenuity of her body.

Mrs. Pluedine is one of the few patients for whom I use the full formal name, rather than a neutral and ubiquitous first name. I often call my patients by their first name with their permission, and I encourage them to call me Alexander. Not all of them are able to do so, possibly because of their upbringing or the proprieties of how to address a doctor. In the case of Mrs. Pluedine, I felt that our mutual use of titles maintained the distance she required to feel comfortable. At the same time, it helped me to impart a verbal respect to her person that I thought bolstered her self-concept as being "somebody." Of course, perhaps I am deluding myself with yet another fanciful theory when the true explanation of her response was much different. At any rate, she seemed pleased and that pleased me.

One of the frustrations of this profession is that you seldom learn what happens next and so it was in this case. I would have liked to have heard more of her story.

# E.   Let's All Play Uproar

I confess that I do not like to do marital counseling. Too often it is not entered into with equal intent or honestly by both parties. I could tell you stories....I refuse to see any quarreling couples without working with a female co-therapist lest I am accused of taking sides. Admittedly, I probably do sometimes show biases despite all attempts to remain neutral and objective. Worse than doing marital counseling, I feel even less inclined to do family therapy, especially by myself. It is like wading through a sea of emotions, cross-purposes, lies, confusion and back alley deals between them that you know nothing about. There is also another reason: Honestly, I am just not very good at it. This remains true despite all of Dr. Harry Goolishian's attempts to train me, and he was an acknowledged expert in this field. But I have performed a few marital and family therapies by myself either because no other therapist was available to take the case or I thought I could do it alone.

The worst example of potential disasters occurring involved a family I counseled in my private practice. The husband and the wife were on the verge of a divorce. His sixteen-year-old son by a previous marriage attended the sessions when he felt like it, which was not often. Their nine-year-old son was for some unstated reason enrolled in special education, and the twin six-year-old girls were always winking and grinning at each other as if they were the only ones who knew what was going on. Maybe they were right.

At one session they had a fight right in my office. I mean a screaming, chair-throwing donnybrook. I was seriously debating whether to call the police and was trying to balance this rather extreme action against the rigid principles of confidentiality. I finally concluded that this was a scene they had played out many times before and I was wise not to be drawn into their drama. Eventually the family members calmed down, or maybe just ran out of steam. One of them finally selected a chair and sat down. The others followed the example, albeit with the husband and wife facing opposite directions and the younger children crying. The sixteen-year-old looked pleased. He was the one who had started the whole thing, and he was the one who had thrown the chair. After this I reminded them of the rules against violence and the principle of talking things out rather than acting them out. Future sessions were equally filled with unpleasant moments even if less action packed. I knew I was not making progress with them and I dreaded each session, but they kept coming anyway. Later I found out why.

After two months of weekly visits, I asked my receptionist if the insurance payment for them had arrived. It had not. When she called, she found that the payments had been mailed to the family's address. At the very beginning of the next session, I asked them about the checks. Finally, less shamefacedly than they should have been, the parents admitted they had cashed them. Why? They were broke and "needed the money." Like I did not? What to do? I could not just quit. Once we begin working with a patient, we feel committed to stick to the bitter end. Patient abandonment is not lightly undertaken in my profession.

My solution was to agree to see them two more times before ending our sessions together, and to provide them with a list of free community-based organizations they could contact for future mental health needs. They promised to forward the next checks they received to me, but they never did.

Two months later the wife called to say that she and her husband were divorced and she was pregnant. She explained that it was her husband, not she, who had cashed the insurance checks and that the family was again in need of help and asked if I would see them. She had not called any of the resources I had recommended. I told her that I was no longer seeing family therapy cases, which was true. I did not of course tell her that this decision was at least partially based upon my experience with her family.

I am still not sure if in this case I should have looked for a co-therapist from the beginning, or if I should have admitted earlier that I was not helping them and then assisted with a transfer to another therapist. It was years before I attempted to work with another family. That is the next case I will discuss and it was my last, for real this time. As I said above, I was just not very good with family therapy.

Regarding nonpayment and financial matters in general, here is an observation that may surprise you: Talking about money with a patient is often much more difficult for many therapists than talking about death or sex or other emotionally laden issues. I leave you to ponder the causes and implications of this reluctance, but I believe this attitude is well-rooted in our society. If you do not agree with me, ask your best friends how much money they make; or consider your own response if you were to be asked this question.

I did not follow-up on the non-payment or to attempt collection of this debt. Psychologists usually absorb financial losses such as these for practical reasons: The patient usually does not have the resources to pay anyway. And, an even more powerful consideration is that when ex-patients are confronted by bill collectors, some become angry and sue for malpractice rather than pay.

# F.  Yakety Yak, Take out the Trash

The title of the 1958 rock-and-roll song aptly applies to a family situation that was one of my least favorite but perhaps one of my most memorable cases. Given my previous experience, I had promised myself I would not take another family therapy case. Why did I accept? Perhaps because someone who provided me with frequent referrals asked me and I did want to refuse them. Why I did not use my rule for family and marital therapy and insist on a co-therapist, I still do not know. Perhaps because my colleagues were too busy at the time or maybe they were just wiser than I was.

The Tremont's were a family, or perhaps in retrospect just a loose coalition, of four people who presented with numerous problems that I attempted to sort out and prioritize.  However the first three sessions with them left me confused as to who was doing what to whom, how, and when. After that it became complicated.

I finally fell back on Harry's wisdom of pulling one string. My naïve plan was to focus on one central theme and the family would miraculously change. The string I chose was one that had been mentioned at the first session: the teenage son's unwillingness to take out the garbage. This was the strong and able lad's one and only chore. Although he did not comply with other household rules, this seemed a reasonable one to begin our work with. It seemed central enough to the family dynamics that it might work. As I developed this family scenario, each member of the family was brought into play. This included the lazy fifteen-year-old defiant son, the ineffective father who seemed to be having a mid-life crisis, the harping slightly younger mother who never followed through on her threats, and the seventeen-year-old sweet, long-suffering daughter who would instead usually do this chore for her brother.

The situation unraveled quickly.  In short order I discovered that the father was cheating on his wife, the mother was a closet alcoholic who slept until noon, the son was not only a belligerent and entitled teen, but a sadistic bully, and the sweet willing daughter was famous for being generous with her "favors" in the back of the school yard. Oh, yes, their therapist was borderline incompetent. Can you see now why I do not like doing family therapy?

Week after week I asked if the son had taken out the garbage at least once. No. Why not? Excuses, finger pointing, shoulder shrugs; I was treated to all of them. I was not able to break the spoke in the wheel that unbalanced the equilibrium of the whole system, but I was determined to keep at it. Not much else got done despite their repeated attempts to create mini-crises to distract me from the goal and drag other red herrings into the mix. They were tired of hearing about the garbage "thing." If that was all I could talk about, they saw no reason to keep coming back. In response I finally issued my own ultimatum: If the assignment was not accomplished by next week, don't bother to return. I informed them it was their decision, but I would not permit them to waste more of my time if they were not serious about change.

This at least brought a solidified response from the family: This was not the reason they had come here in the first place, they had worse problems to deal with that were being ignored, nothing was being done here, maybe what they should change was the therapist, and what was the big deal with the stupid garbage anyway? Yakety Yak.

There is a good rule to follow when making threats: Never make one you do not intend to enforce. As we say in

Texas, I would have been happy to see their collective backsides. But they trooped in the following week, took their seats and essentially said they were finally through with *that* one, the son took out the garbage. What is the next step?

Especially interesting was the change in seating. The father sat closer to his wife, the wife looked less harried, the daughter was by her mother, and the son was isolated and sullen, but risked little smiles on his face when he didn't think I was looking. Not smirks as before, but smiles. Who would have believed it? It worked.

I would of course like to say that they lived happily ever after, but I suspect they did not. They did work harder in therapy and they made some progress on all fronts. After three more weeks, I quit asking about the garbage; they had moved on, at least enough for me to begin thinking that maybe I was not such a bad family therapist after all.

But I knew better.

## G.　The Man Who Cried

I was enjoying a page-turner detective novel rather than catching up on charting during an open hour in my schedule. About five minutes into the book my phone rang and the receptionist informed me that a man and his wife were in the waiting room and they would like to see me. It was not unusual for people to sometimes drop by without an appointment. I would always see them if I had time and concern myself with the formalities later. I went out, introduced myself, and invited them to come in and seat themselves. They stated their names and then waited expectantly. The man was large and powerfully built. He wore casual khaki slacks and a solid-colored long-sleeve shirt, both of which were well pressed. He was either very bald or kept his head closely shaved, which suggested a military background. The woman wore a dress with a subdued flower pattern and had short, stylish dark hair. She instantly gave me impression of a very pleasant person, but one possessing competence and a strong will.

In situations like this where I have little or no advance information about people, I have often found it best to wait and see what develops. The advantage of my silence is that clients usually feel some anxiety and eventually begin to talk even if they had not intended to do so. Our culture does not deal well with large gaps in conversation and, in fact, this is usually described as an awkward silence. In this case the couple may have been under some mild pressure, but it became clear that they thought that because they were now in my office I was in charge and they expected me to begin. When I asked how I could help them, Patricia first shyly looked at her husband and then began. "Guilford needs something to do. Ever since he retired he sits around and mopes all day, or worse yet he expects me to entertain him while he interrupts my schedule." Guilford, who asked me to call him Gill, sheepishly admitted that he was used to activity at work all day and now he was bored. After obtaining some background information, I agreed to see him alone so the two of us could try to work something out.

He arrived punctually for his appointments and things seemed to go well for two weeks. He said he missed a daily routine like he had at the office and at my request he generated a list of activities he was interested in. Bill was what I would call a "Man's Man": very masculine in stereotypic ways and probably had always been very reserved, unemotional and in control. Contributing to this perception was the fact that he had been a Master Sergeant in the Army. It was difficult to get him to discuss his emotions. Then during the third session while he was talking in general terms about his boyhood, he mentioned his father and he suddenly burst out crying. For several minutes he buried his head in his hands and continued with deep wracking sobs. After a while he stopped, looked up and said "I have never done that before." I believed him.

His father had died seven years earlier. Gill described him as a severe alcoholic, undemonstrative except when he was angry, and physically and verbally abusive. He always found fault with Bill and his mother. He degraded both of them and blamed them for any problems that he encountered in life. He never spent even an hour with his son in what today we call quality time. The family was denied things they needed while the father squandered whatever money there was on drinking and his own entertainment. Gill said that, unlike the other kids in the neighborhood, he did not even have a bicycle although he had wanted one for a long time. His mother suggested that he might earn money in order to purchase one for himself.

He cut lawns, ran errands for the neighbors, and saved everything he made. His mother put his earnings in a coffee can hidden in a top cabinet while he kept a record of his progress toward the cost of a bike. Each day as he walked to school, he passed the bike shop and looked longingly at the new Schwinn displayed in the window.

Finally he earned the last bit of money needed and he begged his mother to go with him to buy the bike. She hesitated but finally had to tell him that his father had found the can several weeks before and had already spent the money on drinking. She had been unable to tell Gill this previously. He said he did not cry and, although he became very angry, he was too afraid to confront his father. Much later he was given a well-used bike cast off by sympathetic neighbors, but by then he was too old to ride it and he soon after left home to join the Army. He told me that during his entire lifetime hardly a month passed that he did not think about the betrayal and unfairness of the incident and he still felt the anger. He reported that he now realized that this event shaped who he was today. With little prompting from me, he also recognized that it had contributed to his lifelong mistrust and reserve with others, even with his wife and children. I believe the bicycle event was a symbol of many such betrayals, rejection and abuse by his father, but this one event reminded him of all of them. We finished the work together and he expressed a better understanding of who he was, why he was this way, and how he might modify his reactions and behaviors. He also understood his father better and thought that he might even be on the road to forgiving him. He said that even his wife thought he was "coming around." We parted on a positive note.

Four months later he came in, again without an appointment, and asked if I had a moment. Of course I did. With a great deal of pride he told me that he had solved the problem of his boredom and the situation between him and his wife. They both loved the outdoors so he had purchased two brand new off-road motorcycles. He and his wife now rode together frequently on the extensive, abandoned, old logging trails in the public lands which are maintained by the US Forest Service. He did not mention the bicycle and neither did I, but I think we both understood what a truly elegant solution this was. In one symbolic gesture he had put to rest one lingering pain in his life and solved the situation that had brought him and his wife in to see me. I was most impressed that with the purchase of the two bikes, he had faced the self-limiting problems of his past head on, admitted that it was time to let them go, and moved on. These were new bikes, had motors, and far surpassed any boyhood dreams he could have had.

I was of course a lot younger than he was, but in some way I think he had also found a "father" who could be proud of him, and he had returned to see me in order to show off. Best of all he had done it by himself. To make a bad pun: Sometimes I think my only job is to Kick Start the Process.

# H.    I Love You

This is about a different type of father, but it also ends well. Adam came to see me with a business proposition. He was the owner of a fairly small but expanding business. Being very conscientious he knew that mental health and contentment were not only important to his employee's happiness, but they also minimized internal problems, sick days and turnover.  He approached me about providing employee assistance for his firm. After some limited negotiation I agreed that for an annual fixed price I would see anyone from his business on a totally confidential basis. Therapy would be free to the employee for up to an agreed number of appointments. This could be renegotiated annually as the workforce grew or if too many people began to use the service and it became a problem for either me or the company. The arrangement had been working well for two years when he called me to say he had no idea who saw me, but it seemed to him that the employees were more content and the arrangement was working well. Then he shyly asked if he might also see me. We set up an appointment for him at a time when he would be unlikely to be seen entering my office by anyone who knew him.

Adam and his teenage son Michael were becoming increasingly estranged and this concerned him deeply. He admitted that his work often interfered with time with his son, but he said he always gave the boy "everything he wanted." I suggested that he fulfilled his son's material needs but possibly not his emotional needs.  I asked when he last told his son he loved him. Adam pondered awhile and finally answered softly, "never." I knew his son was involved in basketball and asked how many games he had been to. "None."

He recognized the problem immediately. He said he would make time to go to the games, but as far as expressing love, he had grown up in a family where emotions were not expressed and he seldom even told his wife that he loved her. He did not think he could tell Michael he loved him and he maintained that it was unnecessary because "his son already knew this and he didn't have to say it." I explained it was important to do this first. It was even more important than going to the games or spending more time with him. He said that he would try.

Adam called on the following Monday and asked if I could squeeze him in for an appointment that evening. I did. A somewhat bleary-eyed father related that telling his son he loved him was even harder to deal with than were the feelings he experienced when he attended his own father's funeral. He had not known what to expect, but he finally said it anyway. Evidently the son just looked at him and said, "Okay, that's cool," so Adam didn't know how to interpret his son's response. He did think it would be easier for him to say it the next time.

Adam didn't tell Michael he planned to attend the next game because he didn't want to make a promise he couldn't keep. He did not arrive until the second half of the game due to his work schedule and he was not sure that his son saw him in the bleachers. His son played very well and his team won, both of which made him very proud. When the final whistle blew, the team gathered along the sidelines to form a circle, join hands and make a celebratory cheer. He saw his son look up and suddenly leave his teammates to climb up to the stands. When he reached his father, the son hugged him and said: "I love you too, Dad." Then he went back down and joined his teammates.

They did not discuss the incident afterwards, but Adam noted a warmer relationship between them. He promised his son that he would attend every game that he could. He was so insulated that he had not told his wife about his attempts to be closer to their son, but Michael evidently told her. She was very happy and told Adam that now it was her turn and she expected to be taken to dinner more often and maybe even on a vacation some time. At this point he snorted and asked me, "What's happening? Have you created a monster here?" Then he laughed and said that maybe he was not paying me enough. I agreed, of course, but remained modestly silent.

I continued to provide counseling for the company's employees, but I had no further direct communication from Adam once his personal problems were resolved. The fiscal officer renewed the subsequent year's contract over the phone. As in other cases where I do not hear from clients after counseling has ended, I wonder what happened next.

What I think is noteworthy about this case is how little I really did yet how consequential the change was that occurred. I do not know of any theory I followed or special training I received that prepared the way for this intervention. I simply used my intuition; anyone could have done it. Perhaps the "authority" I held as a professional and his knowledge that I had helped his employees gave Adam confidence that I could help him too.

I hope Adam and his family are well and happy. I wish I could tell them that these counseling sessions helped me too. I learned to tell my own sons that I love them more often, and I went to most of their sports events and other activities.

# I.    The Car Loan

Before relating the next episode, I will briefly review the concept of dual-relationships. There is a fundamental rule in psychotherapy that the therapist must maintain a strictly professional relationship with the client in order to prevent confusion or compromise between the therapist and the client. A therapist must avoid any relationship with patients outside of the therapy session and must not use their position to gain any personal pleasure or advantage. Obviously, you must not sleep with your patients or exploit them financially. Nor should you conduct any dealings with them in which your implicit power might inappropriately influence them. They do not fix your air conditioner or give you a ride home, and you do not accept a free dinner, especially not at their house. You can probably think of other examples. The primary rule of the healer is always, "First do no harm." You may also have heard it in its fancier Latin version, "Primum non nocere." Either way the point is clear.

I have conducted seminars on the impropriety of dual relationships. I have served on ethics committees that investigated alleged violations of this rule and I am especially sensitive to the issue. Granted this becomes sticky at times when grateful patients bring you a small gift or a home-baked treat, so you have to deal with each case individually. You do not give gifts to patients either, especially if they might be misinterpreted. When in doubt, I seek the guidance of a professional colleague, thereby making the contemplated behavior public, not a private event that may be misinterpreted. One good test of many contemplated actions is whether you would do them in public or be comfortable having others know about them.

With this in mind you will read here, and in later cases, of instances where I felt morally and ethically justified in bending the strict interpretation of a professional standard.

Mr. Oakland was a dignified man who always appeared wearing a suit and tie. Both he and his attire were a little old and showed their wear but made a good presentation. He is another patient I always called by his title of mister, never by his first name, even though he had invited me to do so. Given his current reduced circumstance in life, I think he appreciated the courtesy. It may be useful to explain here that I usually let both students and patients decide what to call me. If I am to address them by their first names I feel they have the same right to use mine. Some never get over the doctor title, others seem to like to show off in front of their friends and either emphasize the use of "Doctor" or alternately call me Alexander to demonstrate how well they know me. Mister Oakland always called me Doctor Boeringa.

I saw him sporadically for three years. He did not require therapy as such, just some gentle support from time to time. The basic issue was always the same: He did not want to be put on a shelf. He lived in what in England is called a "bed sit;" here it is just a room in someone's house that includes kitchen privileges. He attempted to remain relevant and earn his own money by selling various products door to door. This provided both a moderate income and some structure in his life, but it created a problem because he could not afford a car. He did not have any credit and was unable to put aside enough money to pay full price even for an inexpensive vehicle. In both the cold of winter and the heat of summer he had to either walk long distances or wait at bus stops and make numerous transfers in order to get to his customers. This concerned me because it was adversely affecting his health and in addition to being inefficient it probably cost him more for transportation than he earned in sales.

I knew another older gentleman who had been a mechanic. He was not a patient of mine but a mutual acquaintance, and I asked him to find a very inexpensive but reliable car for Mr. Oakland, which he did. The problem remained that Mr. Oakland had been able to save only a few hundred dollars for the down payment. This left a balance of four hundred dollars. After much discussion and negotiation I lent him the remainder of the cost and by mutual agreement had him make payments on a modest schedule. My reason for this unusual move was that Mr. Oakland was a man who did not have a mental problem or carry a psychiatric diagnosis. He was otherwise very healthy and only required a support system. His problem was that he had experienced a string of bad luck, not the least of which was falling victim to the demeaning effects of growing old without an adequate pension. The fact that I met him in a clinic in my professional capacity rather than having been introduced by an external friend carried little weight in my decision. I did share my contemplated action with a few professionals who at least concurred with my analysis of the situation and agreed that it was not illegal or unethical. They were only concerned that it might set a bad precedent with other patients if it became known and I did caution Mr. Oakland not to discuss the arrangement with others.

With the use of an automobile, Mr. Oakland increased his sales and stopped endangering his health. Most importantly, he reliably, regularly and proudly paid me back and cleared the debt within a year. What is more, he soon afterwards informed me that he now no longer had time to maintain our appointments because business was too good. About six months later, he even offered me a ride home in his car when he stopped in to see me. As he was now officially not a patient, I accepted.

To this day I have tremendous respect for Mr. Oakland and feel privileged to have known him. I am sorry that he is not able to read of my high opinion of him and the affection in which I held him, but I heard several years ago that he had died.

## J.    The Whiners

In every setting that provides services of any kind there are always some "customers" that are well known, uniformly disliked, and often referred to internally by the initials PITA. You can guess the full meaning. For those who need a hint, the first initial stands for Pain. There may be a higher percentage in mental health settings because of the very nature of the emotional and cognitive problems the clients experience, but at any rate, they exist in significant numbers. In this case, I had just started working in a new location and as the new guy on the block I was assigned a number of such patients. I suspect some had been recently and most gratefully transferred from the rosters of other clinicians. Faced with being stuck in a room with them individually for an hour each I resorted to forming a group of what I considered to be the worst offenders. It had an official designation that I think was the Medication Group or some other neutral sounding term, but privately I called it the Whiners Group. Admittedly, this was not very nice of me and it contradicted my often-stated belief that I could find something to like about every patient I saw. During my initial private meetings with each patient I had found little to support this assumption. To be honest, I had a bad attitude and perhaps I was a whiner too.

There was Mr. Simms, a sallow and sour looking soul who if he ever had a kind word to say about anyone he kept it to himself. Ms. Fansing or Gloria, as she liked to be called, was the queen of past glories that never were. She hated anyone who had ever wronged her and evidently that included everyone, particularly men. Mr. Glass literally and verbally whined that no one liked him. During the time I spent with him, he enumerated almost every slight he had ever endured. This all continued in a high-pitched voice that with private amusement I began to think could indeed cut glass. By the end of the session I had silently added myself to the list of those people not liking him. Mr. Anthony had dirty stringy hair and his physique defined what it meant to be obese. He answered only in monosyllables and drooled copiously. I later learned that this was not from any medication; he was not on any. His life was also defined by "slings and arrows of outrageous fortune." The list of patients continued to an even dozen.

Every week for an hour-and-a-half each group member competed to outdo the others with new complaints, indignant recitals of prejudicial treatment in all quarters and the meanness of others towards them. Included were their relatives, "supposed" friends, and employees in the store where they shopped for groceries. If I were to believe them, their doctors were the worst offenders of all. I supposed by extrapolation that I was already on or soon to be added to the list and probably ranked near the top.

Now that I had these people in my care I did not know what to do with them. As I read the long histories in their voluminous charts and discussed them in clinical rounds with their previous therapists, I found that most of the standard therapies had already been attempted and none of them had worked. After a few weeks of group sessions, it became clear that I was not helping these people either; I was starting to dislike them and I dreaded each meeting. This was not a good situation for them or for me. I began to wonder how they had become so negative; surely they had not been born seeing the world through s--t colored glasses. In final desperation, I told them that we would hear the life story of one member each week. To avoid any bias I wrote their names on pieces of paper and one name was randomly drawn each week. They would have the floor and, while others could ask questions, there were to be no comments or personal interruptions while the featured speaker was talking. It brought an excitement to the group, with the suspense of who would be called. It was like winning the lottery and they looked forward to it with eager anticipation.

And so it began. Each person had the opportunity to talk as long as they liked during "their moment of fame" and afterwards we would discuss either the presentation or current issues of the members. There were few rules except that if you responded you had to say something supportive or nice. Their stories were often fascinating. I saw each individual in a new light. Caught up in their own history they did not whine, well not as much anyway. The audience was surprisingly respectful. They sometimes made connections with their own experiences and, I think, began to like each other a little if for no other reason than for seeing something of themselves in others. I found myself liking them more as I began to understand them better and to see them as complete persons rather than as their symptoms. Mr. Simms showed some compassion; at least he did in his response to those in the group. Gloria remembered some good times in her life and often had the group laughing. Mr. Anthony told her that she should have been on the stage. He seldom drooled and he seemed to sit up straighter. And when Mr. Glass heard some nice things said about him, he beamed. Now I am not Pollyanna, and it was not as if a magic key had been turned and all was perfect in Whiner Land. They were still people with serious problems and a history of behaviors that were not easily reversed, but it was a start. I actually began to look forward to these group sessions, a sentiment which, when stated to the rest of the staff, had them rolling their eyes.

On one occasion I was faced with copying, collating, and stapling a large number of study materials for a seminar I was scheduled to give on the next day and I had been delayed until the last moment while awaiting a missing article. What to do? I needed at least three hours to accomplish the task by myself, but group was about to begin. I did the "unthinkable" I asked the group to help me do it. I know, I know, this touched on both dual relationships and exploiting patients. Wonder of wonders, they not only agreed but they all worked together as a team and took pride in being able to do so. They arranged an assembly line themselves and completed the job in forty-five minutes. They exhibited a great deal of excitement while engaged in the process. My thanks were genuine and, independent of the needed help, I felt this had been the best group session we had spent together. Evidently so did they. After that I did not exactly look for work for them to do, but when one member noticed that a table in the waiting room was wobbly, he decided to fix it. One man went to his car to get a few tools and, with the advice and assistance of everyone, the table was quickly repaired. They had a purpose.

By the time I left to take a new job I was genuinely sorry to leave "my" group. They threw a surprise farewell party for me and I noticed at least the hint of a tear in a few eyes, including mine. It was not too difficult to transfer the group to another therapist this time. The bad reputation of the members, while not completely gone, was at least considerably ameliorated. Once I was in my new location, the group at their insistence made a conference call to me that we both enjoyed. I knew that continued contact would not be fair to their current therapist, to them or to me. It was my last contact with them.

# V. THE FUN ONES

My clients had varying degrees of serious problems though they were all painful for them or they would not have come. Sometimes their distress would threaten to weigh me down as well; it was difficult not to identify with them. It was then that I learned not to take my work home with me. I did the best I could for these patients and then, as a wise police officer once told me, I "left it at the curb." In various ways, however, most were a joy to work with. Many of them I came to love. The memories of these people still have me smiling or laughing as I recall them.

## A.   My First Patient

In graduate school I was expected to apply what I was learning in my academic classes and to engage in a several-semester-long *practica* at one of the local mental health facilities. My first assignment was at the Austin State Hospital where severely mentally ill patients are treated on an in-patient basis. No real orientation was offered, and when I arrived there on my first day of training, I was assigned to one of the units of the many wards on a seemingly random basis. I was expected to work several days a week depending on my class schedule. A secretary issued me a badge and a few keys and directed me down the hallway to my designated unit. I was then on my own.

After a little fiddling with the keys, I was finally able to open the heavy metal door and enter the large day room area. It was filled with patients, many of them wearing hospital garments but some of whom were in regular clothing. To my knowledge, I had never before seen, much less met, a mentally ill person. Certainly I had never encountered them in such large numbers. The austere nature of the hospital and doors that locked from both the inside and outside intimidated me only slightly less than the patients I saw. They seemed to be randomly sitting or wandering around and some of them appeared to be talking to themselves or making strange gestures. I had no idea of how to put into practice any of what I had presumably learned and I just stood there wondering what to do. Finally a nurse came up to me. She said "Go ahead and pick one honey, you can't hurt them." I am not sure if she meant that nothing I did would further injure them, or if I was probably so inept that I could not do anything to help, much less harm them. In medicine and the helping professions the primary law is, "First, do no harm." I thought I could at least observe that dictum. To be honest, I was still somewhat frightened of the patients and was concerned whether I had acquired sufficient skills to help them.

The nurse's words, however they had been intended, gave me courage and I walked over to a man who was sitting by himself and looked harmless. I politely introduced myself and asked if I might talk with him, but he did not respond. In fact neither that day nor on any subsequent day did I ever see him move from his bench except when he was gently guided back to his room or to the cafeteria. As a rule, he did not utter a word to me or anyone else. I finally surmised that he was what we called catatonic, but by then I had already chosen him. Since it is not in my nature to reject someone or potentially hurt their feelings, I "kept" him. His name was Harold. Sitting with him in silence gave me an opportunity to more closely observe the activities of both the patients and the staff. By the end of my workday, I grew comfortable enough to initiate conversations with a few other patients. I was also less concerned when other patients approached me, even if was just to ask if I had any cigarettes for them.

I did eventually see patients who were more verbal. A few of them had been there for a long time and evidently took it upon themselves to mentor the various young students who came there for training. They would initiate a conversation by asking if you were a nurse, social worker, or psychologist and then ask what school you were from and how long you would be at the hospital. When I seemed not to have a clue about what to do next, they even gave me a few hints. As old hands they knew the ropes.

Many of the patients were probably bored as there was not much for them to do. They sought out anything to break the monotony. I came to believe that many of the patients assumed that the primarily reason students were there was to amuse them. For entertainment, their best catch was to snag a lawyer, but there were few opportunities for this. Second best would be a visitor who smoked and could be talked into sharing. My guess was that psychologists and social workers ranked lower on the list. One patient began a conversation by asking if I would like to hear about his sex life. I actually did, but I thought it more polite at the time to say I did not, and he seemed disappointed. Evidently, many of the students accepted his offer. The staff told me that he had great stories, even if they varied each time he told them. Some of the patients seemed so "normal" to me that I would check to see if they had keys and were employees. This was important information because as students our greatest prohibition was to let an inmate out the door. The key, pun intended, information to remember was that the non-patients were the ones who already had badges and keys.

Harold, my mute patient, continued to abide in his stillness and I continued to visit and sit quietly with him. Sometimes I might comment on the weather, or muse as to what he might be thinking, but mostly I matched his silence. He never looked up when I arrived or seemed to notice when I left, but I continued to maintain what I thought of as my commitment to him. During spring break I missed two weeks of our sessions. I did not tell him beforehand since he did not seem to hear me and I had no indication that he even noticed my presence. When I returned, he was in his same place as if I had never left. I walked up to him and sat and after about ten minutes I distinctly heard a voice gravelly with disuse ask: "Where were you?" and then, "I missed you."

That was not to be the opening of a flood of words or a brilliant cure unleashed by my therapeutic persistence. He never spoke again, but it encouraged me to maintain my

85

silent vigil with him until the end of the semester. I believed he was aware of my presence and that he heard me. That was enough; how much more can we hope for even in a friend. When I finished my semester and before I left, I told him goodbye. I touched him for the first time by patting him gently on the shoulder. I was truthful when I said I would miss him, but true to form there was no response, only perhaps a small flick of his eyes as I walked away.

Several years later I was sent by the American Psychological Association to visit the Austin State Hospital as an accreditation examiner for the psychology training program. Of course I looked for Harold, but it seems he was long gone.

You always remember your first.

# B.   A Day's Outing

Long before I became a psychologist, I had an interesting experience with a patient from the Austin State Hospital. It may be difficult to believe, but at one time it was possible to hire the more functional psychiatric patients as day laborers. Many patients routinely worked on the hospital grounds doing landscaping and other chores for minimal salaries. Others were allowed off the grounds for the day to work for anyone who was aware of this possibility, even contractors. The patients would usually then perform unskilled manual labor in the community for very low hourly rates. If a rationale was required, I suppose that this came under the category of "Occupational Therapy."

My mother-in law at the time thought that this was helpful to the patients, as indeed in some cases it might have been, assuming that they were not exploited. I think that she and my father-in-law had previously hired patients. I was helping them out with some chores at a rental house they owned. Evidently she decided I could use help so she called the hospital and arranged to have one of the patients work with me for a day. The job would be to clean windows and pick up some trash. I would complete some house painting that I had begun the previous week.

When I arrived at the Administration Center, Eddie was waiting for me. He was dressed in work clothes rather than hospital pajamas and he was carrying a bag that contained a lunch the cafeteria staff had packed for him because few of the "employers" wanted the added expense of feeding their workers. From the grin on his face, it was apparent that he was pleased to go outside the hospital grounds for a while and to earn a few dollars. He was friendly and he chatted excitedly as we drove to the work site. Once there I carefully explained the tasks we were to do together that day. He nodded his head enthusiastically to everything I said. To be fair to Eddie, he did try but he was not the best worker, and was easily confused by the tasks. By noon he had washed one window, badly. I asked him what he had for lunch and he dejectedly held open the bag so I could see the single, sad and boring institutional-style sandwich inside. We threw that away and went to a local restaurant where I bought him a lunch of his choosing. I treated each of us to a beer later that day since it was very hot outside. A friend advised that I not include this little bit of history or at least change the beverage to a soda. You decide. For me, the statue of limitations has run out. Either way, he really liked the chosen refreshment. He did slightly better at cleaning up the yard in the afternoon, but he continued to be easily distracted. He frequently would drop what he was carrying to pick up a leaf or twig or other object that held more interest for him. I decided that it really was not important for me to manage him more closely; neither was it my task to improve his work habits or try to teach him new skills. I just let him enjoy what he was doing.

We returned to the hospital at the end of the day. I thanked him for his help, and when I paid him, he assured me that he was available to work with me ANYTIME. Looking back on the experience, I think it was a good day. I enjoyed the time with him too.

## C.   Wilma

At another hospital where I was a student, I was assigned Wilma, a patient with a diagnosis of schizophrenic disorder. She wore a wrinkled and somewhat stained shift and had frizzy white hair flying everywhere, and whenever she smiled, it was apparent that she was missing at least half her teeth. As soon as she saw me enter the ward, she rose expectantly and took a few tentative shuffles in a pair of worn flip-flops. When we met, I introduced myself and told her I was her new therapist. I suggested we talk and get to know one another. She immediately began complaining loudly of a variety of injustices she felt were inflicted upon her. Chief among these was that she was not given any independent privileges and she never received a pass to go off the unit to the patient commissary like all the other patients. Her doctor did not think she was "ready." She hoped I would understand how unfair this was and I would intervene with her doctor for her.

I knew this physician and was aware that he had obtained his medical training in Mexico. I know there are several excellent medical schools in Mexico that are attended by highly qualified Americans who are unable to get into American schools. In addition, I have worked with many FMG's or (Foreign Medical Graduates) and found them to be excellent clinicians, both competent and compassionate. However, I had never heard of this school and when I asked him about, it he informed me that few Americans attended it because the classes were taught in Spanish. Based on this information, when I met him in the parking lot a few mornings later, I greeted him with "*¡Muy buenos días! ¿Cómo está usted?* " His response was a seemingly confused "What?" My Spanish and my accent are not great, but they are not *that* bad. A subsequent inquiry of a Spanish-speaking aide confirmed that the doctor was not competent in that language and she had frequently been called upon to translate for him with patients. His main qualification seemed to be that he had a medical license. Period. It is sometimes difficult to recruit physicians to work in mental hospitals, but I hoped not that hard.

At any rate, Wilma was severely lacking in interpersonal skills so one of the things I did to help her was to coach her in improving her social repertoire. I practiced with her how to enter into and respond to conversations and we role played using polite phrases such as "Good morning, how are you?" In English, you will notice. Then I asked her if she liked compliments. Oh yes, she loved them. Well, didn't she think others might also? She guessed so. I told her that the next time she saw her physician she was to tell him how nice his tie was and see if he did not appreciate it. We did a role play together and went over these lines a few times until it sounded sincere and spontaneous. The next morning as she waited in the line to see him for patient reviews, I surreptitiously observed. When her turn came, she greeted him appropriately, evidently for the first time, to which he responded with some surprise in his voice, "Well, good morning to you too, and how are you today?" She then perfectly dropped her rehearsed line about how attractive his tie was. He almost gasped, smiled broadly and then stood, pulled up his trouser legs and pointing downwards asked, "And how about my new socks? I just bought them yesterday." Flustered she just stood there not knowing how to respond to this, but he hardly seemed to notice. Later when I saw him, he told me how much she had improved lately. He thought it might be a change in the medicine he had given her and he remarked that he had written her a pass for that afternoon. I heartily agreed and then quickly left to hide my laughter.

Wilma of course was very pleased and, while I will not exaggerate and say that she became a social butterfly, she seemed to be more open with people and less negative in her attitude generally. She was generous with her compliments to almost everyone including staff, other patients and even occasional visitors. In return I think that people were kinder to her. There was not much I could do to cure her underlying disorder, but she certainly learned something useful to her and went on to practice it well.

Good on Wilma!

# D. The Prostitute's New Life

One of the things I enjoyed about working at a hospital was the variety of patients I was able to interact with. Some of the more "difficult" cases were often relegated to my care, especially when I was a student or a relatively new staff member. These were sometimes the "frequent flyers" that seemed to come and go in the hospital through a revolving door, but more often they were the personality disordered and troublemakers. One example was a female patient assigned to me who possibly suffered from a schizophrenic disorder, but she might also have just been the unfortunate result of a mixture of a horrendous childhood and various psychological and emotional disabilities. Whatever her diagnosis, any grossly abnormal behavior was usually well controlled by medications. She was however very streetwise and clever and this led to multiple conflicts with society's rules and institutional policies. The best example of this was the fact that while in the hospital she was denied off-ground passes. In response, she would periodically climb the low wall surrounding the hospital and escape to what she called her "vacations." She was young and reasonably attractive and could easily make her way to the nearest truck stop. She was always picked up by drivers who probably thought they had hit the jackpot.

The problem was that after a few days without medication her less attractive symptoms would assert themselves and her liabilities became more apparent. Apparently, in their response to this new development, most of the truckers tried to be gentlemen. They would usually pay for an extra night in a motel and then sneak out early the next morning. By now tired of her vacation and with no money of her own, she would go into town or just sit by the side of the road. If this did not work, she would begin to rant and rave at people or steal something from a local store. Eventually some police officer would pick her up. She would tell them where she "lived" and they would provide transportation back to the hospital, where she stayed until she again became restless.

At an earlier time in her life, she worked briefly as a prostitute. Somehow, the man who had been her pimp learned that she was at the hospital and he came to visit her. It did not take long for him to convince her to return to him. On the other hand, maybe she convinced him. Either way, he swore that this time it was not to be as a working girl but as his wife. She then asked me to help get her released from the hospital.

I met with the boyfriend twice and he seemed to be either an excellent con man or genuine in his feelings for her, maybe both. Legally she was not a danger to herself or others and there was no way the hospital could keep her if she wanted to go with him. The problem was that she was white and he was black and this was the South during a time when fierce prejudices were very much in evidence. Several of the staff were outraged at the thought of their relationship and they strongly urged that she be committed if this was what it took to keep her apart from him.

My analysis of the situation was that independent of any other considerations she was free to go and that outside the hospital chances were that she faced a better life with him than without him. Given her previous track record, she obviously could have left any time she wanted to anyway, but it seemed important to her, and to him, that they do this "legally." In fact under the law, there being no compelling reason to keep her hospitalized, releasing her was certainly the "least restrictive alternative" for her. The fact that this occurred during a period of so-called "dumping" when state hospitals were trying to discharge as many patients as possible probably influenced the decision. Everyone reluctantly agreed on discharging her.

She left, but not without creating a few bitter feelings toward me by some staff. They characterized my intervention in these actions as immoral and, given the time frame, what they probably thought of as evidence of communist leanings. It seemed common in those times (and in some places still is) to characterize any deviation from what some people consider to be the "straight and narrow" as evidence of communism. My opinion was and is that there is already too much unhappiness in the world to contribute to any more of it if it can be avoided. This woman found her own way to the freedoms she valued and I think she enjoyed life more than many people do despite the limitations nature and culture placed on her. I wish her, and the man, who probably really did love her, well. I hope she is happy. I think of how many people never have the courage to make the situational choices that could ease their own misery. She at least tried.

# E.   Never Trust a Little Old Lady

Prior to the introduction of effective psychotropic medications, many mental hospitals were in fact bedlam, the word being coined after a twelfth century London hospital for the insane by that name. Bodily constraints, overcrowding, long periods of isolation in unmonitored cells, wrapping in wet sheets, and a long list of ineffective terrors were once common. In more modern times the indiscriminant application of Electro Convulsive Therapy (ECT), otherwise known as Shock Therapy was used on a broad spectrum of mental disorders. A sidelight on this is that I am actually a cautious advocate of ECT as it is sometimes employed today when it is medically indicated and more mildly administered in a well-regulated form. I have personally witnessed its effectiveness with some depressed patients for whom no medications seemed to help. The once popular film *One Flew over* the Cuckoo's Nest is not totally factual, but it dramatically portrays some of the abuses of the twentieth century, including ECT.[5] Prominent then was the use of seclusion or the popularly referred to Rubber Room. Please understand that there is sometimes a legitimate place for what we now call the "quiet room" or some other euphemistic label. Use of such a room is sometimes the last resort against impending violence, and it is a kinder method for out-of-control patients than using restraints. Some way must be used to keep both patients and the staff safe from harm. Patients who feel they are losing control may even request it.

---

[5] *One Flew Over the Cuckoo's Nest*, film based on novel by Ken Kesey. Written in1962. The film was directed by Milos Forman, and produced by Saul Zaentz and Michael Douglas in 1975.

Focus on patient rights was gaining momentum and the abuses of prolonged seclusion were legally identified and addressed. New regulations were being formulated to provide appropriate safeguards. Obviously since this was going to happen anyway, fact finding about current practice could guide the future of informed decisions and stricter guidelines.

I was once present when a delegation from a legislative body came to investigate possible abuses at a local mental hospital. The staff at this hospital had assiduously and compassionately limited all forms of unnecessary restraint and they adhered carefully to the rules for placing someone in isolation. Frequent documented observation occurred and strictly adhered to specific time limits were being followed. However, the visiting committee had been officious and bullying in their investigation all along and clearly their demeanor and harsh questioning indicated that they believed that crimes were being committed and they were going to discover them. They traveled in a tight group and seemed to glare at the staff. They spoke with employees only when it was completely necessary. I must admit I took an immediate dislike for them and enjoyed my own amusement at what happened next.

When the committee members came to an isolation room where a little-old-lady patient had been placed, the ward staff dutifully recounted the careful considerations that had been taken before placing her in the room. They tried to present the records that detailed the conditions of use and the documented frequent observations, but these were brusquely swept aside. The investigators were hot on the trail of suspected abuse and a cover-up. Why was this frail woman being subjected to this treatment? Without even first looking through the window to the seclusion room, they imperiously waved the papers aside and demanded that she be instantly released. They would determine the situation for themselves.

A nurse obediently unlocked the door and, as it opened, the 98-pound woman sprung out and took two of the committee members to the floor. She then began pummeling and trying to bite them. We observers of course stood by, not wanting to interfere in any way with their investigation. After the horrified third member of the committee finally screamed that something had to be done, several staff members reluctantly pulled the patient to her feet and restrained her. The charge nurse could not resist asking if they still wanted to talk with the lady and, if not, could they return her to the isolation room. I never did learn her name and I do not know what demons drove that woman, but I still smile at her pluck.

As a closing note I was doing a little research for this case because, in fairness, I wanted to be sure I did not overstate my comments about previous conditions and the lack of effective treatment of mental patients. It seems I did not exaggerate conditions. I encourage you to explore this on Google, etc. yourselves. Notwithstanding the wonderful, humane and compassionate treatment I have most commonly observed, it seems that some abuse continues. Of course there is no excuse for this, but please also consider that these are, I hope, fairly rare. For the most part, the people employed in these facilities receive low pay, little chance of advancement and sometimes work in extremely difficult conditions. They do the best they can.

# F.   Junior

Violence, for many of my patients who had this propensity, was a major obstacle to their functioning and comfortable survival in open society. Such was the case with Junior who got into frequent fights. So far his arrests for this were relatively few and the charges against him fairly minor. However, it was only a matter of time before he seriously hurt someone, went to jail for his behavior, or both. His father had also been a violent man who not only beat both Junior and his mother, but was also a drunk and a philanderer. Junior once told me about waiting near the tavern his father frequented and then, to provide for his safety, following him when the tavern closed. His father did not go home, but instead visited his latest girlfriend. Junior sat outside her apartment all night waiting for his father to come out so he could ask him to please return home. He finally fell asleep. Only the early cold morning dew awakened him and caused him to abandon his vigil.

I understood how much of his history might contribute to the almost constant furnace of anger within him. I believed that he began to understand this as well and we were making some progress. Along the way I began to notice a frequent common element in his stories of fights with other men: Junior was an African American and his opponents were always white.

After a while, he was able to verbalize the fact that his angry combative lifestyle was not a productive way to live and he too saw the need for change. I risked the interpretation that he might be redirecting the anger he felt for his father toward those he attacked, and that what he really wanted was to beat-up his father. Because he was afraid to do so, he displaced the anger onto other men, and specifically onto white men since he felt that they also subjugated and humiliated him. It was like the proverbial light bulb went on; he could see how this might be true. With some trepidation, I then asked him if he noticed that I too was white and an authority figure. He laughed and said, yeah, but I was safe, he liked me. I hoped this was true.

One day I had an appointment with Junior and I called in to tell my receptionist that I was running late. She said she hoped I was okay and not sick or anything. It was then that I foolishly explained to her that I had yet another quarrel with my neighbor because he had thrown beer cans and other trash over the fence into my yard. Why she, in direct violation of office rules, shared this with Junior, I do not know, but she did. When I finally arrived and we were seated in my office, the first thing he said was: "You know, Doc, I could beat him up for you." I of course told him that this was the kind of problem in his thinking and behavior that we were trying to eliminate to which he protested: "Yeah, but for you I would be glad to. I like to beat people up!"

I would be less than honest if I said that in fantasy I did not at least consider his offer. We continued to work on his anger management and he did stop getting into fights. We finished our work together and as so often happens I did not hear from him again. I did later read in the paper that he had changed his job and was directing his energy to working with a civil rights organization, one based on the principles of non-violent action, I was glad to notice.

# G.  My Very Own Gang

One of the ways in which I sometimes earned a little extra money was to provide psychological and intelligence examinations for eligibility determinations by the Social Security Disability Board. These were usually fairly routine tests and I was well practiced in the administration of the standard instruments involved. The write-ups were brief and mostly based on objective scoring. I would generally have applicants come in the evening or on a Saturday morning to my home where I maintained a small office with testing materials and adequate privacy. However, I was paid extra if I was willing to do home visits with those applicants who were incapacitated or did not have transportation. Several of these people lived in a low-income housing area and when I received the first request to visit someone there I had some concerns. It was in what was clearly a rough area and one mentioned frequently in news reports of crime and quite often the latest outbreak of gang violence. This immediately assumed a special relevance in my thoughts.

As I drove up I could see several young men standing in a tight knot along the curb. They had clearly spotted me long before I saw them. They drifted closer as I opened the car door and I knew that with my suit I was probably pegged for a warrant server, a bill collector or a repossession man. As you might imagine, none of these were particularly welcome in this neighborhood. I braved it out and greeted them pleasantly while all along trying to keep the thin quaver out of my voice. Sullenly they asked my business and I said I was there to see Mrs. Appleton. "What do you want with her?" The threat was clearly implied and I was too outnumbered and not physically equipped to fight back and too slow to run with any hope of making it back to the car.

Besides, I had accepted this assignment and I knew from the reports I had received that for her claim to be considered this lady sorely needed the information I was here to collect. I patiently and earnestly explained my role, including the potential benefit to their neighbor, when they broke out into grins. At the time I thought they seemed to believe me, or perhaps they were aware of my purpose in being there from the beginning and were just having a bit of fun with me. Or both.

"Oh, you are here to help her then?" "Yes," most emphatically, "yes." "Then let us escort you." There was the clear implication that they would protect me from whatever other dangers might lurk.

I sat on Mrs. Appleton's sagging sofa and tried to ignore the blaring TV which, after asking her three times if we might turn it down, I just accepted the noise. There is a good chance she did not understand some of the simplest of questions I was asking her. I did not get very far into the testing when it became apparent that her cognitive facilities were severely diminished. As a psychologist I could only give what factual data I had and not offer any medical diagnosis, but my non-professional guess would be that she was fairly far advanced in Alzheimer's Disease. I could only speculate about how she functioned on her own. I did ask her a few questions about how she got along. She said that her sons came to see her "sometimes" which by her tone I took to mean seldom, especially when she said they were busy too and she understood. Then she brightened and added that of course some of the boys in the neighborhood got her groceries and helped in other ways when she needed them. "Maybe you met some of them on the way in?" I think that cinched it for me whether they were expecting me and just having fun or not. When I left her house, my escort was waiting for me by the door.

I visited the projects several times to see other applicants and each time the young men would seem to already know I was coming, and they would meet and courteously escort me to my client. I even stopped in once when I happened to be close to the neighborhood to see if Mrs. Appleton had received any news about her entitlement. This time they clearly did not know I was coming and it caught them a little off guard: my own little bit of fun with them. Aside from teachers and the law, I think I was perhaps the only professional these men had met. They were curious about me and had many questions about what I did. After we became more accustomed to seeing each other, we often stopped to talk when I was in the neighborhood. They asked what a psychologist is and how you became one and other questions about a world of which I think they were totally unacquainted.

I don't know if they were really a gang. Perhaps today they would call themselves "homies." I think that for a few hours they were my homies too. I hope so. I wish now I had spent more time talking to them. I also hope that their briefest of contacts with me perhaps influenced their future in some small way for the better. Who knows? I also hope that Mrs. Appleton received the financial help she needed but, again, who knows? The experience with "my very own gang" taught me not to depend too much on stereotypes, but to be more open and not as judgmental. That being said, I was still glad they considered me in a friendly manner.

# H.   Pick-Up Sticks

I had a part-time position at an inpatient facility serving children and adolescents. Because it was quite distant from my house, I would usually stay over for two nights in a spare hospital room that was provided for me. That arrangement freed the travel time (three hours each way) for me to work the extra hours and to help fulfill my part-time obligation at the facility. There was still no way I could see all of the patients I wanted to work with one-on-one for even an hour each, but the extra time gave me some contact with all of the patients albeit on a limited basis. I also maximized my time there by providing training to the staff, teaching them a little about theory and presenting some practical applications. My hope was to extend my ability to reach more children by creating knowledgeable, effective co-therapists who could apply the basic principles of counseling and behavioral intervention.

The first time I set up a class I insisted that everyone who worked with the patients attend, even the director. When at the beginning of the first session I noticed that the cook was not there, I sent for her. The messenger returned saying that she would not come. I went to talk with her and she protested that I really did not want her; she said she was just the cook. Eventually, although reluctantly at first, she came and sat through the classes. She was too shy to ask questions, but I noticed how attentive she was and how at times she would nod her head as if in agreement or understanding. In observing her in the dining area, I noticed too that she had an innate understanding of how to deal with the children and with people in general, perhaps gained through her experience with her own eight children and many grandchildren. We would sometimes talk together after the tables were cleared and the dishes were done. It was then that she asked her questions, soaked up ideas and presented some of her own wisdom. She became my best helper, support and co-therapist. I also received extra helpings of pie at meals. A fair trade-off.

Soon after a talk to the staff about overcorrection, I had an opportunity to demonstrate it. Overcorrection is the process of having someone engage in a repetitive correct behavior as a consequence for having displayed an inappropriate one. It helps to repeat an intervention several times in order to change the old, unwanted behavior and instill a new, more adaptive one. You don't just fix it, you continue the fix until it is clear that you finally "get it" and are probably not going to do it again, at least not if there is a possibility you are going to be caught. Either way you at least know how it should be done. So when one teacher came to me with a crisis, I immediately responded. "Johnny" had thrown pick-up-sticks all over the classroom and would not clean them up. Rounding up a few other teachers as observers, I hurried to the classroom. There I faced a small defiant boy who, with arms folded and face red, repeated his refusal to me. Clearly he had done things like this before and had gotten away with it every time. The implication in his stance and tone was, "What are you going to do about it?"

Fortunately it was soon lunch time so I had all his classmates dismissed except him. As they filed out past him I could see looks in the other children that suggested everything from curiosity to horror. Johnny appeared a little apprehensive, but it was clear that he was not too worried; he had faced bigger battles than this. The teacher remained but stayed in the background with her colleagues to observe. The heat was on me. I told the boy that if he picked up the sticks before lunch ended he could eat, but if he did not pick them up soon he would miss not only lunch but the following playtime as well.

His response was to try to leave. I was bigger than him. I sat in the doorway and blocked his exit. If he attempted to play with toys or otherwise ignore me I would repeat my directions and firmly redirect him to the task, physically if necessary. After two hours he reluctantly picked up one stick. I praised him for it and piece by piece, with praise for each advance, he slowly picked them all up. He had already missed lunch and the other children were just now returning from the playground. I had them directed to another classroom.

As soon as he finished he looked expectantly at me and headed for the door thinking he could finally leave. He was probably hoping for a late lunch. Instead, I took the tube of sticks and again scattered them all over the room. He was, I think the term is, flabbergasted. I told him, "Now please pick up these and then you can join the other children." I won't say that he leaped to the task, but eventually he did pick them all up, but not without some crying and a lot of muttering about unfairness.

There was no immediate magic transformation in him, but we actually became good friends in the weeks that followed. Additionally it was reported that his general cooperation improved both in the classroom and in other areas as well. When his parents came to visit, they noticed the change. The word spread through the staff that maybe this guy knew what he was doing.

I was gone the next two weekends and returned to an excited childcare worker who could hardly wait to inform me that she had used my techniques and was very proud of herself.

One of the children had thrown food in the dining room and created a huge mess. I was hoping to hear that the teacher had made the child clean everything up and then repeat the cleaning the next day as well, perhaps even for the next week as the child was older. But no, she told me she marched the girl into the play room and threw the pick-up-sticks all over the floor, then made her pick them up twice. She stood there waiting for the praise that she had expectantly waited for since accomplishing this intervention.

How to explain? The cook would have known what to do, but she was off for the day. I was at a loss. This lady was trying so hard; how could I not at least praise her for her initiative and then help her to better understand the principle? I do not remember what I finally did, but I am sure that it was gentle. Learning sometimes follows a crooked path.


Two Added Notes:

(One) When I present a term or a theory that I think might be misused or misunderstood by the reader, I check it out in one of my books or on the internet. I did this for the concept of overcorrection to ensure other sources support my understanding in the event my readers think what I did was a little weird (perhaps it was) or they want more information. In this case I found some good material that I think is well presented. Since the internet changes so often I will not give a specific URL, but I feel reasonably certain you can find something if you are interested.

(Two) Some of you may be thinking "why were the parents not consulted first," why weren't Informed Consent forms filled out, and why was there not a case conference first held, a cooling-off period instituted, and optional interventions exhausted? Finally, what were the rights of the child and did he have an advocate?

No to all of them.

With respect to the usefulness and sometimes even the necessity of my using these measures and others that might be open to question, I think that most professionals can and should be trusted to use their educated and well-considered judgment as long as it is unlikely to lead to immediate or lasting harm. I think that this case meets that test. You may not. Just so you know that I am not ignorant of the alternatives.

# I.   The Other Side of the Street

Patients often project both their positive and negative feelings onto the therapist. This is called transference and it can be useful in working through some issues such as feelings towards a parent or lost lover. Patients also idealize their therapists (I give an example later) or even over identify with their therapists to the point of thinking they love them. More about this soon. At some point in therapy, I often ask patients how they feel about me. As you might guess, few people have ever previously been confronted with such a direct question. It shocks them. Some of us might not ever ask it being unsure of what the answer might be and not willing to confront the truth. I think that it is often a reasoned and sometimes necessary question.

Understand that just as there might be a positive transference there can, and often is, a negative transference as well. Either one can be useful of course, but they can also get in the way or elicit unrealistic projections or expectations that have to be dealt with in therapy.

I have had several homosexual patients and of course I frequently ask them the same question. "How do you feel towards me?" One of my openly gay patients responded by asking me if I meant was he sexually attracted to me. When I affirmed that this was one possible feeling option, he said definitely no, I was not his type. I confess it upset me a little bit; it always hurts to be rejected. Even when you want to be.

This same man sometimes cross-dressed and on more than one occasion, he came in drag and drenched in cheap perfume. I told him that it gave me a headache and that the last time he did this I had to keep the windows open for the rest of the day. He just giggled and said, "I'm sorry Doc, I just feel like such a bitch today!" But from then on he did back off a little on the industrial grade fragrances. The women in the office frequently made snide remarks about him, but they always envied some of the very stylish and expensive clothing he wore. One of the other staff members told me as a whispered aside that this was because he looked better in the outfits than they would have. This is obviously a remark that I was too smart to repeat.

By the way, his reason to see me had nothing to do with his sexuality; he had no interest in changing this aspect of his life. It was never an issue that, outside of his perfume use, was ever discussed. He came because of relationship difficulties with his partner. It seemed that, in spite of his occasional use of female attire, he was the dominant one in this pair and recently "she" (as he referred to his partner) had begun to push for more freedom and resented his bossiness. Sound familiar? He finally asked if he could bring in his girlfriend because with these issues it might help if they were in therapy as a couple. Of course I agreed.

A week later I was walking down the hall and right in front of me I noticed a pert figure with long blond hair and a very cute and wiggly butt in tight jeans. My thoughts and possible fantasies at the time will remain censored. I am sure you guessed it already. When the person turned around, I noticed it was the "girlfriend," also obviously a male, who had come to visit. Sometimes a little retrospective denial can be useful. I think I am fairly secure in my "masculinity," but this is still the first time I have told the story publically.

Because I basically am comfortable with many forms of diversity and am not generally judgmental, the word spread in the gay community that I was a good therapist and a safe person with whom to disclose issues. I saw many gays and a number of same sex couples in my practice over the years. Today I would refer to these patients as LBGT (lesbian, gay, bisexual and transgender). I am still a little surprised, but I suppose I shouldn't be, at how the relationship problems of couples in this community are so similar to those of straight couples, and how they correspond to many of the problems I have personally experienced as a heterosexual. Couples fight about sex, money, and family, with power struggles involved in all three categories. I guess there are only so many ways to screw up a relationship and I hope I learned to avoid at least some of them. Obviously not all, I am divorced and have other broken relationships scattered over the years.

You do not have to be perfect to help others with their problems, just able to do so. I think if you thought you were perfect it would be a great impediment in your practice and probably more so in your life. Fortunately, I have had spouses, friends, lovers and most of all two children who remind me at intervals--and sometimes at great length--about each of my shortcomings and failures.

One night in the ER, I was notified that a potential suicide was being brought in. A crowd of noisy people entered in a great rush and stampeded down the hallway, almost filling my tiny office. Some of them were too drunk to walk well, but they still tried to support the distraught patient. He was male but they all told me simultaneously to call him "her" and to address her as Desiré. Everyone tried to explain all of the problems at once and each grew subsequently louder. I thought a fight was going to break out. What eventually became clear was that she was threatening to kill herself and had made serious attempts to do so in the past.

After I sequestered the Greek chorus in the waiting room and the patient in my office, I learned it was the same old story of unrequited love and cruel rejection. Her dress was wrinkled, her hair in a bird's nest of confusion and her lipstick smeared to a red streak. One shoe was missing. I listened patiently to a weeping, disjointed account of a seriously dysfunctional relationship. I had frequently heard similar stories from patients and sometimes even from friends. She eventually promised not to kill herself, and to return the following day for an appointment with me. As I wrote the appointment slip and made sure she knew where the clinic and my office were, her friends yelled in unison that they would make sure she got there on time and reassured me they would all see me later. I hoped not soon. One such encounter was enough. The next day Desiré missed her appointment. Another common occurrence.

# VI.    THE YOUNG ONES

I was tempted to label this section "Give Love a Chance." You may wish to do so after reading it. I value the opportunity to provide counseling and positive intervention in the lives of young people. They have a chance to make changes before their personalities, habits and lives become solidified, and they have a longer time to enjoy a life with the gains they have made.  If they are open to growth, love and forgiveness can make a tremendous difference in both who they are and who they become. Many of the young people I counseled seized the opportunity. They made a decision to change and were able to accept the help offered them and turn their life around in a very short time. The alternative was a life of continued pain and bleakness. Those stories are brutally sad. I like to think that the people I was unable to help were able to reevaluate their lives at a later date and use the suggestions and tools I gave them. I was always on their side. I tried to impart to them that they deserve more from life than they had received and it is their right to try, and continue to try, to find some happiness.

## A.   Give Kids a Chance

The following stories involve several different children who influenced me.  They are brief, but I would like to share them with you.

I have a reasonably broad training in psychology, but I am least qualified in child psychology and neuropsychology.  Because those fields require very specialized knowledge and skills, I make referrals as needed. I have a friend, Patricia, who is a brilliant child neuropsychologist.  I wish I had had the opportunity to refer patients to her when I was counseling children. Early in my career, when I thought I knew everything, I provided parents with basic, academically-acquired parenting information and techniques.  That was before I had children of my own. I decided soon after becoming a parent that I should search out each of those parents and apologize to them.  I had no idea how difficult parenting could be or how silly, impractical and presumptuous some of my textbook suggestions were.

Less than a month after my first son was born in Galveston, I witnessed a scene while walking to a waterfront restaurant where I planned to have lunch. That memory still haunts me. A very poor and possibly homeless family was sitting on a door stoop. The child, about the same age as my son, was lying on a dirty blanket spread over the hot sidewalk. He looked lethargic. He did not cry even though the hot sunshine on his face must have made him very uncomfortable. I reflected on how different the lives of the two children were and probably would continue to be. Even assuming they received equal love and care, my son would grow up in a completely different world. Chances were slight that this child would benefit from the same privileges and opportunities I would be able to provide my sons.

The doctors-in-training I supervised in the Mental Health Emergency Room several evenings a month often preceded their Psychiatric rotation with one on Obstetrics and Gynecology. They always had many interesting stories from that experience. Most students were young and they loved to tell their stories late at night when business in the ER was slow. They were often awed that they had delivered a baby and they recounted the wonder of this event and the pride they felt at being able to present the child to its parents.

Other stories had equal wonder but were not so joyful. They told me of one girl who, when given her baby to nurse, told them to come back later; she was watching her favorite soap opera. She had no interest in the child. To top them all, one student said he was wheeling a thirteen-year-old girl to the delivery room when she asked him when they were going to put her to sleep. He explained in lay terms that they might give her a mild sedative or spinal block, but there was no need for a general anesthetic. Frightened by this she asked "They're not going to cut my belly open while I'm awake are they?" He assured her there was no need for a cesarean, whereupon she demanded: "Then how's that baby going to get out of there?" We all laughed and someone asked the obvious question: Did she have any idea of how the baby got in there? However, it was a nervous laugh. I think all of us were considering the plight of both mother and baby and how long it would be before the baby of this baby had her own child and what the future of either of them might be.

While I was in college I did volunteer work at a school for mentally retarded children. No matter what their condition was, I quickly observed that regardless of their disability they had parents and staff who obviously loved them and gave them excellent care. It was greatly rewarding to me to come into the facility and be greeted by exuberant welcomes and heartfelt hugs from the children.

Once we went on an outing to Brookfield Zoo. They enjoyed themselves enthusiastically, but I noticed that other visitors were stopping to stare or were covertly whispering to their own children, probably telling them not to stare. I thought with some annoyance: "What are they looking at?" Then I looked again at my charges and realized that oh yes, I was so used to them I no longer noticed: My group did look a little strange. I guess that without habituation I would have stared too. Compared to some children I encountered in the community, I knew they had a great life and I was lucky to be a part of it.

Years later I thought of this as I sat with a fifteen-year-old in an adolescent hospital and heard his story of being hated by his parents, and the repeated abuse and rejection he suffered by being a "throw-away child." I thought also of a fourteen-year-old girl whose mother wanted her out of the house when the mother's frequent boyfriends were around. The mother admitted that she was jealous of her developing daughter and feared competition from her. This girl turned to alcohol, drugs and promiscuity and was subsequently hospitalized for acute alcohol dependence. When the mother came to visit, she took her daughter for a drive and as they pulled away from the curb showed her two six-packs of beer in the back seat. "You know you are going to drink again, you might as well start now," was the mother's explanation.

The girl returned angry but sober and asked me what sort of life I thought awaited her. What answer might you have given?

I also saw a nineteen-year-old boy in therapy that lived on his own. When I asked about his parents or any family, he just shook his head and refused to say anymore. He was shy and had few social skills. He told me that his work did not require him to interact with anyone and I was often the only person he spoke with all week. I tried to put him in a group, but he refused. Then I practiced simple conversation with him using role-plays of common interpersonal situations. I encouraged him to repeat this with store clerks or anyone who might be bored or have time enough on their hands to be pleased with some company. He reported that he did this, but his story was not very convincing. The last time I saw him I was returning from emergency room duty at 1 a.m. He was alone, head down, wandering near the railroad tracks. I did not, in fact could not, stop. If he lived he would be in his fifties today and I wonder what his life is like. I hope my guesses are wrong and that he has found some happiness.

## B.  Motorcycle Lady

My personal, completely unscientific belief is that at least eighty-percent of the "bad" kids I have seen in therapy are the direct product of a rotten environment and truly bad parents. I also believe that a few kids are born "bad to the bone" and the result of twisted genetics. Even some animals are born with emotional problems. Still, I know of few dogs that are naturally mean. They may be bred to be aggressive, but it usually takes training to make them mean. It is not much different with people: Most behavior is learned.

One of my patients was referred to me by court order in response to her substance use problems. She had a history of frequent overdoses which led to emergency room visits, and she repeatedly "failed to engage" in prescribed treatment plans. For some reason she continued in my counseling sessions for a while but not for long. She was a self-described "old lady" to a motorcycle gangster. It seemed apparent to me that she was getting some value out of therapy as she used the time well and stayed beyond the sentencing requirement. I learned among other things that she was expected to earn a set amount of money each night and if she did not she would be beaten, and that with her old man's permission she might be passed around like a dope pipe. Beyond that, she would not say. In fact, she confessed that she had probably already said too much.

One day she made her most surprising confession: She wrote poetry. At my request, she shared some of it with me and said I was the only one to have ever read it. It was often ungrammatical and I do not know if it was good in a literary sense, but it was certainly moving. I cried. That is probably still a big no-no for therapists, but I was suddenly overwhelmed and could not have stemmed the tears if I had wanted to. I do not know what she thought of this. Maybe it scared her, but I think it went deeper than that. Our relationship had developed a modicum of respect, trust and truth, which she may not have experienced before. On a level beyond predictability, our worlds had established an intellectual, and to some extent an emotional, connection. I think her newfound openness frightened her, limited though it was. It was not a world she could continue to live in and we both knew it. I was concerned she would not return to therapy so I asked her to come to one more session. She did but she was tight, uncommunicative and seemed afraid. I heard a clunk when she put her purse on the floor. Was it a gun? Yes. I don't think she brought it to hurt me but, instead, as a reminder to distance herself from therapy. She could not, from her point of view, economically, emotionally or socially afford to better her life. For me the outcome underscored that that she lived in a world I would never really understand and she chose to return to it. Perhaps she had a glimmer of understanding of a better life but did not believe she could achieve it. The sad part is that she may have been right. She left halfway through the session, rapidly.

Did I cry? No, but I felt like it.

## C.    The Actor

A principle in psychology called the Zeigarnik effect states that unfinished actions are remembered better and have more drive to become finished than those that are competed. The point is that unfinished or unsuccessful cases stick in my memory and are more easily recalled. There were also many successes among my patients, and while I celebrate each of them, they do not stand out as starkly as the "ones that got away." The next is a good memory.

A little boy was referred to me by his pediatrician to see if I could do something about his intense shyness. It took the first session for him to stop looking at the door where his mother waited in the next room and stop asking if he could go now. By the second session he was a bit more relaxed but answered in monosyllables or not at all. Play therapy brought little progress, but he at least began to tell me his fantasies. They were mostly about the quite un-shy actions of superheroes and child actors he had seen on TV. Having little idea of where to go from here, I began by asking him how he thought grownups should behave. He did not know. What happened next had to be either a brilliant intervention or just a stupid idea born of utter frustration. I followed up with the question: "Should they behave like this?" and I climbed on a low set of sturdy, wide shelves that surrounded the room, made outrageous noises, scratched like a monkey and in general acted like a complete fool. He sat in open-mouthed wonder. I think if he could have run from the room screaming, he would have. It would probably have been the most prudent thing to do actually, but he stuck with the program.

Fortunately, my receptionist was off that day or she certainly would have come rushing in to see what the

119

problem was and I would have had trouble explaining it to her. I also hoped his mother, whatever she heard of the sounds, might think it was all routine behavior. I think at first he was frightened, then curious, then he began to giggle, and finally he roared with laughter. He pointed and screamed "More! More!" Of course I obliged and then eventually stopped and told him it was his turn. All reluctance was gone. Like a train slowly picking up speed, he climbed onto the table, threw a few things around the room, and made all of the kid noises I believe are in every child's repertoire. Finally we both collapsed laughing. I asked him if, when he got home, he could show his parents what grownups should not do and he agreed. Before he left I cautioned the mother as to what to expect and assured her that it was all part of the treatment and she and her husband could enter in if they wanted to.

The end of the story is that from then on he began to talk more with me during each session, and together we invented more sedate homework for him to do at both home and school that would help him be less shy. He began to come out of his shell with other children and then even with adults. After awhile we mutually agreed that he had "graduated" and did not need to see me anymore. I was sad to see him go but knew that this independence was best for him.

The sequel was when some time later I received an invitation to a school play in which he was a minor actor. Of course I attended and brought my own children. When I saw him deliver his lines with such comfort and assurance, I felt very proud of him and told him so afterwards. During the performance in the darkened theater, I may have shed a tear of happiness or two, but I will never admit it. Notice that I do not use a name for this boy even a made up one and again this is purposive. I can share the events but as a real person his memory remains my own.

## D.   Look at Me

A physician and I co-taught third-year medical students the basics of patient interviewing. We used role-playing as one method to teach techniques, after which we critiqued the students' practice interviews. We tried to instill elements of respect and common humanity that would be reflected in their interactions with future patients. I think most students came to medical school with high ideals and the excitement that they would soon be allowed to relieve the suffering of others and to cure diseases. They wanted to help others. I believe, however, that by the third year their idealism was pushed to the back burner by horrendous work and study loads. The instructors made incessant demands on them, not the least of which was the expectation to instantly know everything and to always be right. Of course I could be wrong, as I was never subjected to the process and was just an observer, but I thought I saw a steady slide into their becoming "gods" over the years and the tendency to see patients only as "the gallbladder in room B203." It was that attitude we sought to combat.

About this time I coincidently saw Rose, a twenty-two-year-old woman who had experienced the ravages of a cancer that left her without a nose and with other damage to her face. She was coping with all of the multiple impacts of this and handling the implications of her disease quite well, better than I might have. Her one complaint was that people did not really look at her anymore. She was assured that eventually she would overcome the disease. Then the plastic surgeons would begin reconstructive surgery and her face would return to its normal appearance. But this would be a long way off; forever to a twenty-two-year-old. Meanwhile the prosthesis she was given to wear only drew more attention to her appearance. She felt that no one in her life listened to or understood her feelings.

Her parents only saw through tearful eyes how pretty she had once been. Her friends, the few times that they visited, looked at anything in the room but her. Worst of all, she said, were her doctors who no longer saw a person but a disease. Many of her care providers were medical students and residents near her age but they did not treat her as an age mate with shared interests. They focused on only a small part of her: her nose. They did not see her as a person like them and this hurt her immensely. Perhaps it was too threatening to the students to recognize how much they were alike and how by only a small degree they had escaped the perceived distance between them. For whatever reason, this was a particular source of pain and annoyance for her.

She wanted to say to them "Look at me!"

I asked her if she would like to have the opportunity to tell them her thoughts. She accepted the offer and she spoke to the students at our next interview class. She did not wear the artificial plastic nose covering she had been given. She repeated her observations and made her request directly to them: "I am not a missing nose; I am a person like you. In different circumstances you would like to know me, and I am really not so different from you now." Look at me!

Only an insensitive person would not have been moved by her plea. Rose effectively conveyed the points that my colleague and I had been trying to make all term much better than we had. I would like to be able to report that all was well after this, that her caregivers were swayed and responded as we both would have liked, but she was transferred to another unit.

I was struggling with a heavy caseload, the demands of research projects and a newborn son at home. In short, I lost contact with Rose. If the person I describe should read this, I would appreciate an e-mail letting me know that things did turn out well for her and that she is now, as she was then, truly beautiful to look at.

# E.   The Doctor

A young woman who was very conflicted about her studies came into the student health center for assistance. She was trying to decide whether she should continue in the university. As we talked she sat nervously twisting a handkerchief and looking around her as if the answer might be pasted on one of the walls or the ceiling. The more we talked the more it became apparent that her concerns were not academic but personal. She was from a small farming community some distance from Austin and her hometown boyfriend objected to her going to the university and being so far away. He was jealous of the men she might meet in college and insecure about their relationship. He was a high-school dropout with a low paying job as a mechanics assistant and he sometimes supplemented his income by driving a tractor. On weekends he would come see her in what she described as his bright-red pickup with twin chrome exhaust stacks. She said that most of the time they had together was spent having sex or arguing about whether she should leave her studies and return home to get married.

It is a basic premise of mine that I am there to explore the issues presented to me and to assist the person in making their own decision. Since it is not my life, it is not my place to tell anyone else what to do with his or hers. After much deliberation and soul searching, I violated that principle and told her that all other choices were of course hers, but she should start using birth control immediately and she should refuse to have any further sexual intercourse without using it each and every time. Long story short, she followed this advice. By the way, lest I be criticized for my recommendation, I was already aware that birth control did not conflict with her religious beliefs. The next time I saw her she said that she had followed my advice and had gone directly from my office to a health clinic and "got on the pill." She added that she had a big fight with her boyfriend and she did not think that their relationship would last much longer. This seemed like a relief to her and she stated with conviction that she would continue her studies and did not think she needed to continue counseling.

Four years later I was on the faculty of a medical school and making my rounds in the hospital when, among a new group of students, I saw her looking directly at me. Shyly she asked if I remembered her and whether we would have an opportunity to talk. I did and we did. Thankfully, it was a slow day for a change when we met and we talked for hours. Unnecessarily but generously, she credited me with making possible the long road she had traveled to this point of entering her medical studies. She told me that soon after ending our sessions her boyfriend gave her an ultimatum of quitting school, or else. She rejected this choice and he dumped her. Within a week he was dating a local high school girl. She could barely suppress her giggles when she said that the new couple was now married and expecting their third child. She stayed in college where she excelled in pre-med. She was accepted at the University of Texas Medical Branch, and she was here for her first year of studies. Not too surprisingly she said she was considering a career in psychiatry, but she would see how things turned out. I was pleased that her experience in therapy seemed to have helped even though it was an unorthodox suggestion that made all the difference. She was "kinda" dating another medical student, but she smilingly assured me they were using precautions.

You do win a few sometimes. I felt good about her, and about me.

# F.   Toilet Training

Well, we might as well get this one over with. It is not my most pleasant memory of doing therapy even though I do consider that it was a surprising success. Jerrold, a thirteen-year-old boy was hospitalized for extensive tests for various genetically-related developmental and mental disorders. He was referred to me to correct his problems with enuresis and encopresis, i.e. incontinent peeing and pooping. As you might imagine, these problems at his age were particularly disturbing to his family although he seemed relatively unfazed by them. A urologist examined him completely and determined that there was no physical or neurologic cause. Due to Jerrold's mental age, I began with play therapy as in his case a nonverbal approach seemed the best to try. He was encouraged to use the various dolls representing possible family members however he wished. Experimenting with the clay quickly became his favorite activity. My task was to closely observe him with a minimum of verbal intervention and to figure out what was going on in his life and relationships. It did not take long for a hypothesis to present itself. Neither did it require a Freudian psychoanalyst to interpret his behaviors. He frequently rolled clay into long thin forms and gleefully pelted the parent-like dolls with them. He poured water on each of the family figures.

At this point in my career I was not well versed in behavioral modification techniques and had seldom used them but, given the one or at most two-week stay projected for this boy, I knew I had to get a move on (no pun intended).

My research of the literature led me to a book by Azrin[6] and Foxx called *Toilet Training in Less Than A Day.*

This seemed wildly optimistic, but I resolved to try it. I certainly didn't have any better ideas.

With the help and support of the staff, I provided multiple opportunities for Jerrold to use the toilet by offering him copious supplies of soft drinks and as much food as he wanted and then insisting on frequent practice sessions. In brief, the interventions for the most part consisted of interrupting his play, which he did not want to do, then instructing him to walk to the restroom by himself, drop his pants and sit on the toilet. If he did urinate or have a bowel movement, he was still required to sit there for a minimum period after which he could pull up his pants and return to play. If by chance he managed to void, he was taught to "finish the job," including washing after which he was enthusiastically rewarded, often by more drinks or potato chips. It was a vicious but productive cycle guaranteeing multiple opportunities for random successes. If he ignored the signals that he needed to use the toilet (and we were assured by his physicians that he did receive them) and he soiled himself, I instructed him to practice. In a neutral, non-judgmental manner I insisted that he had to change his clothing and rinse it himself. Then he would change into fresh clothing without assistance from me or the other staff. He was then overcorrected by more practice of interrupting play and sitting on the toilet. I tried to make a game of it as if this was just a very normal part of activity and emotionally neutral. Obviously he was never scolded and there were no failures, only opportunities for more practice. So far we had only experienced wet pants.

---

[6] Nathan H. Azrin, PhD and Richard M. Foxx, PhD, *Toilet Training in Less Than a Day* (New York: Pocket Books, 1974).

The crux came about noon when he had a bowel movement in his pants. He was extremely disgusted at having to remove the soiled clothing, wash the solid materiel out in a tub and clean up after himself. By contrast, I praised him when he later had a bowel movement on the toilet. Staff throughout the facility and other kids gave him high fives and enthusiastic support. He had never received such accolades before and was beaming. Even his favorite hero, GI Joe, was proud of him! If anyone, including visitors, had not yet heard of his success, he made sure that they were informed.

He was reliably toilet-trained by the end of the next day, exceeding my highest expectations and wildest hopes. A miracle. In the following days he had only two accidents and he clearly showed how disappointed he was by this. One occurred when he could not reach a toilet in time. His explanation that it wasn't his fault and that he had tried was quickly accepted. The other happened only a day earlier and I think it was a test. The training was briefly reinstated and he got the message.

Please be assured that this was definitely beginners luck. I am not convinced that it will work this easily if I ever do it again nor do I guarantee it will work for you. As the disclaimer one frequently sees on packages or hears in television ads states, "Your experience may vary." For Jerrold this was heaven. For the first time in his life he didn't need to be stuffed into diapers to be a welcome participant on bus rides and field trips. He became a well-accepted playmate in sports and games at recess.

When his parents came to take him home, they were pleased with his rapid progress. I carefully instructed them in the procedures to be continued and in the methods that had to be used in order to maintain the new behaviors. I cautioned them that a return to old situations and possibly poor relationships within the family would almost certainly precipitate a rapid return to old habits. I stressed this point because they did not demonstrate warmth to Jerrold during their visit but instead paid more attention to their two older children. They bragged to people they met that their oldest son was a football player and their daughter was a cheerleader. They were however thrilled that Jerrold was "housebroken." (My wry term for their weak response, not theirs.)

Less than two weeks later they called and were clearly deeply distressed: "He's doing it again!" and following close upon this: "Will you take him back?" I asked several questions and surmised what had happened. On a recent Saturday there was an important out-of-town football game. During the previous week, they had "naturally" needed to focus "a little more" on the roles of the football star and the cheerleader than their other son. It was not stated specifically, but the parent's description and tone suggested that perhaps they had been a little forgetful in following Jerrold's reinforcement regimen since he came home. On the big day everyone was dressed and ready to go when halfway to the car, guess who had a huge bowel movement.

"Of course," continued the parents, both speaking on separate phone lines, "that ruined everything." Mother had to stay at home to clean Jerrold. Then he said he felt sick and might have another accident so Mother missed the big game. The father volunteered that it spoiled the whole weekend for him and his children. I do not think Jerrold's feelings were mentioned or considered in this recitation. There was nothing useful I could say, nor did I trust myself to say what I was thinking and feeling. They lived some distance away and so, after an appropriate amount of listening, I promised a referral to a child psychologist in the area and hung up. I do not feel very good about the way this turned out for the parents or for Jerrold.

This was another case of the operation being a success but ending badly. I know that the parents were basically good people and I understood how difficult it must have been for them to accept this less-than-perfect child whose accomplishments they could hardly brag about. If I could have spent more time with them, I think I might have helped them accept both Jerrold and themselves as they were. I would have liked to try.

As a footnote: When my own children were learning to use the toilet, I basically let nature take its course, letting them proceed at their own pace but praising them for their successes. I had no interest in a 24-hour turnaround and certainly neither did they. The fact that I cannot remember anything more specific about their toilet training suggests they sailed through it without trauma on either of our parts. (Sorry guys for even mentioning it).

# VII.    THE SEXY ONES

Sex and violence are themes that sell in any media. Perhaps I should have included more stories containing those issues, but they are not always the ones that bring people to therapy. Very often these problems are just the symptoms even though they may appear to be the primary concerns. Presenting complaints in marriage counseling are usually related to sex, money and family issues. The underlying problems that accompany these usually run much deeper. The point is that even if by magic I were to be able to fix the sex problem instantly, the rest of the problems would still be there.

Another aspect of sex entering into therapy is that sometimes patients really do "fall in love" with their therapists. The relationship is, after all, a very intimate one between two people. Often the therapist is the only person the patient knows who is, or has ever been, "nice" to them. Think now, how often has anyone ever listened to you for fifty minutes at a time? That is, without interrupting to tell their own stories? Moreover, with unconditional positive regard for you? Not often? Me neither. Whenever an attractive female patient seems to be developing a strong positive transference (as we like to call it) to me, be assured that I do feel the tug. I also ask myself if I were to meet this same person under different circumstances, say at a bar or at a party, would she still be as attracted to me. Usually the answer is a clear and ego shattering, "No." That dose of reality helps keep things in perspective. Later I will relate the story of a woman who told my wife how wonderful I was. Without looking ahead, you can probably already guess how well that went over.

There is a disagreement among mental health workers as to whether it is ever acceptable to have a relationship with an ex-patient. Surprisingly to me, there are even differing opinions among a few mental health types who think sexual liaisons with existing patients are acceptable. I will let you decide this. My rule has always been a clear "No!" in both cases but timeframes and other circumstances may cause differing opinions for others. I have friends who are married to ex-patients and it seems to work for them. Who am I to judge?

I do recall the time an attractive woman who had been my patient six months earlier called and invited me for a drink. Although I did not accept the offer, I must have felt strongly tempted as I immediately called my current supervisor and discussed it with her. She agreed it was a bad idea. The fact that she now knew about this and I would certainly be quizzed about it during our next supervision session was an added safeguard should the woman call again. She did not.

# A.   Honesty

This is a story I like to tell on myself to students. I think it is instructive for them as well as a good reminder for me. When I was a fledgling psychologist, I interviewed a very attractive young woman who was wearing a white, very short and very revealing, thin spring dress. Immediately after the interview my supervisor invited me into his office. He had seen the woman in the waiting room and I think may even have assigned her to me on purpose. His first question was what my feelings were for her. Yes, the much overused and annoying question we so frequently throw at patients, and should not. "How do you feel about...?" Intentionally misunderstanding, I said that I thought it was a simple case of test anxiety that could easily be helped with. He asked the same question again and I answered that three or four sessions should be enough to resolve the issue. This time he leaned forward and asked a bit more pointedly, "How do you **feel** about her?" Unthinkingly I blurted out, "Oh my God, I wanted to go to bed with her." And as you probably understand, this is the cleaned-up version. I thought my career in psychology might be over, but he laughed and said, "thank goodness," if I could not have admitted this he might not be willing to supervise me. Assuming that if I could not even recognize in myself a completely normal response to such a powerful stimulus, then I was either not insightful enough to be a therapist or I was a complete liar. Neither one was acceptable to him in a student. He then told a story on himself which not only helped to further relieve my tension, but also allowed me to see him in a different and more human light. And no, I will not be sharing that story with you. Students tend to idealize their teachers and supervisors as much as patients do their therapists. There will be more on this theme later.

I believe that it is vitally important for therapists to explore and be in touch with their feelings, needs and prejudices and to be honest about how these might impact their work with others. In this case, if I was unconsciously trying to impress or seduce this woman, how much would my feelings interfere with therapy? A lot, I think. The fact that one has feelings and impulses does not mean that we have to act on them. This is as good an injunction for therapists as for patients. In fact, if I were in denial it would certainly interfere with my perception, effectiveness and even my motives in doing therapy. As another example, if in working with homosexuals I unconsciously hated them or was concerned about my own sexuality, any attempts to help them would be biased. For this reason, it is beneficial for therapists to undergo their own therapy. Know Thyself. It was a good precept a few thousand years ago and is still relevant today.

A useful rule is to take your own emotional temperature first and if it is rapidly rising, figure out where the heat is coming from. Confront yourself first and then the patient. Some, but not all, feelings and fantasies may be originating from you, not the other person. Later in my career the principles of being aware of my own responses, not letting them interfere, and certainly not acting on them helped me in several situations.

The other half of the equation is that, having been trained to be sensitive to others' feelings and emotions, I sometimes picked up feelings in patients that they had not yet become conscious of. When I detected fear, anger or sadness, I knew that although the patients might not have been aware of their intense emotions, they would be influenced by them and the feelings would eventually be expressed. If the patient wants you to know that what they are feeling, they will eventually find a way to tell you. Keep listening. Do you think this concept relates to the next case?

# B.   Beth

Beth was a middle-aged woman whose two children were grown and currently living in different cities some distance from her. They were not close to each other and seldom even called, much less visited. Her husband had recently divorced her and now he was often seen openly making the rounds with a number of younger women in the small town where they both lived. She was feeling not only humiliated but also old and unattractive, and was deeply depressed. She knew she needed help and on the admission form she wrote the reason she entered therapy was "to get her life back." For much of the first two sessions she cried, blamed herself, and spewed hate for her ex-husband and the "sluts" he was now dating.

I make a point of noticing as many things about all my patients as I can. In this case, I noticed that she was an attractive woman and had maintained a good figure over the years. This did not mean that I was attracted to her, just that I was aware of this. I was also aware that, probably due to her current distraught state, she was neglecting her grooming and was wearing unflattering clothing. She was noticeably calmer by the third session and for the first time had taken some care in her dress and grooming.

The next sessions were primarily focused on how understandably lonesome she felt and how living by herself had changed her life. While describing all of the things that she missed in her present situation, she somewhat casually introduced sex as being one of them. Harold and she had always been very "active" and this was one of the reasons she could not understand his leaving her. Then she continued, "I suppose now that he is single again he is screwing anything that moves; but where does that leave me?" Just in case I missed this, she followed up by complaining that, after all, she had needs too. Without going into more graphic detail she left no doubt about the nature and extent of those needs, and her frustration at their going unfulfilled.

Gentle reader: Are you beginning to get the picture she was clearly painting? And what do you think might have been the intent? Whether it was done consciously or not, she was being coyly seductive. A subtle invitation was clearly presented. And, yes, my emotional temperature was rising and now unbidden pictures were beginning to form in my own head. As I stated above, one of the principles of therapy is to be aware of one's own responses, to not let them interfere, and certainly to not act on them. I did not yet confront her but knew that soon I had to point out what she was doing and get the therapy back onto a more productive track.

I need not have worried about waiting for the opportunity to bring the subject up. When she arrived the next week, she was noticeably braless. I immediately confronted this and asked her what she thought her behavior might mean. Initially she attacked me for my "dirty mind." She said she had a right to dress as she pleased and, by the way, " I'm not wearing any panties either; so what?" When I failed to react to this and persisted in my focus on her intent, she eventually admitted that she had always gotten her way with men by seducing them. She was able to verbalize that, when in previous sessions she had been flirtatious and I failed to respond, she felt rejected. Also she panicked somewhat. The rejection increased her fear that all men might reject her now that she was a little older and not quite as attractive. With more discussion, she realized that she did not want to face her issues of living alone. In fact she attempted seduction to avoid facing other issues. She hoped to distract me with this last effort.

After that she stopped being flirtatious and began to work on the problems she came to solve. As the weeks went by, she became more independent, liked herself better, and was getting her life back. She developed friendships with a few women and while she still hoped to find a new mate, it was not such an urgent matter. By mutual decision we were able to terminate therapy sessions. I soon took a job in another state. I did not know what developed next in her life until I received a letter from her a few years later. She informed me that she had recently re-married and was enjoying life with her new husband.

# C.  Trust

A variant on the last story is this one about Rhea, another woman who hated her life as it was and yet desperately tried to avoid making any changes. At the same time, she knew she needed help so she accepted therapy and the option for change it provided her. She had many conflicted feelings, each slowly pulling her apart. In a more literal sense than for Beth, her life might really have ended. She had already made several suicide attempts that were almost successful. These were not "gestures." In the last one, she misjudged the potency of some pills she took and came close to dying.

Despite her pain, her resistance to making significant changes took many different forms, each more inventive than the last. She often arrived late, missed appointments, insisted that whatever I asked her was unimportant and refused to answer, and frequently scolded me for being a lousy therapist. She also tried seduction, something that she had used in the past to avoid a problem or distract from the issues facing her. According to the history she provided, she used her sexuality to avoid situations that made her uncomfortable. She was accomplished and persistent in avoiding responsibility for her behavior. As she was a very attractive woman, she had no difficulty attracting both men and women and had frequent stormy, short-term relationships. When the tensions in her life were too uncomfortable, she would cut or injure herself or attempt suicide.

Given her history, it was surprising that although she often was drunk and overdosed on prescribed medications, she never abused non-prescribed drugs. She explained this by saying that they were sinful. I accepted her logic, but did not understand it. I was just grateful that her rationale prevented her from using street drugs.

Rhea was my patient for more than a year and in that time we went through many crises together. Therapy went slowly, but there was always some small progress that encouraged both of us to continue.

Once after working through an especially difficult issue from her past, she began crying. This lasted for twenty minutes when we were at the end the session. Considering her frequent attempts to erode any of the limits I had set, I needed to maintain the mutually agreed upon constraints of our sessions. I gently told her that our time was over and I would see her next week. I offered a box of tissues and reminded her that she could use the empty office next to mine to compose herself. I then stood and held the door open for her to leave, which she eventually did, very slowly.

The next week she stormed into my office "loaded for bear." She screamed at me, called me several names that I had never been called before and stated that I was a terrible therapist and a disgusting and uncompassionate human being to boot. I was sure that any moment my officemates, alerted by the loud commotion and the potential for violence, would soon be bursting into my office to rescue me. I think it was only because they knew the patient and had heard yelling from her before that they stayed out, but were prepared to come if I called for help. When she calmed down sufficiently, I asked her to tell me why she was so angry at me. She sputtered out that no other person on the planet would have kicked her out so coldly as I had done when she was so distraught during the previous session. They would at the very least have tried to comfort her and offer her a hug. I then asked her what would have happened if I had let her stay the extra time or given her a hug.

Without missing a beat she looked up at me and said: "I would never have trusted you again."

In explaining the necessity of limit-setting to student therapists, I have often offered this episode as a cautionary tale. It was equally instructive to me at the time. This episode occurred fairly early in our work together. We continued to have regular sessions for nearly a year until we both agreed that there was little more to gain. By then Rhea was basically a much happier and well adjusted person. She would be able to deal with new problems as they arose without the help of further therapy; if she could not, I would be there. For a few years I received what she called status reports and then I did not receive any more letters.

I wish I could have told her how similar everyone's problems are, and how much I learned from her and from our work together that benefited my own life and my maturing as a psychologist. I admire her courage in facing her demons and her persistence in changing her life for the better. I honor her as a person. If she reads this and, even with the many walls and disguises used to maintain her confidentiality, she believes that she recognizes herself: Know this is true.

# D.   How Many Times?

I once worked as an adjunct therapist in a sexual dysfunction treatment group. Some of the couples had never consummated their relationships even after several years of marriage. Many participants had impotence or vaginismus; almost all had pathological shyness, basic ignorance of human sexuality or several other problems. Among the services offered was a weekend workshop of individual training and interventions for a variety of sexual problems. These sessions were conducted at a local hotel and were staffed by physicians, psychologists and social workers. They included individual physicals as well as "home work" assignments carried out in the privacy of the patients' rooms. All segments were followed up on by a team who would review the patient's progress. Close to "graduation," sexual enhancement aids and sex toys were introduced to the entire group. This was always a high point of the session, with giggles and gasps by all.

As one of my duties as a facilitator rather that full-time staff member, I would review a pre-workshop questionnaire with participants. This sometimes proved more embarrassing to me than to them. On one occasion I interviewed an unaccompanied woman in her thirties. She was very shy and nervous. She seemed concerned about what questions I would ask her and confirmed that I would not share this information with her husband. I intended to put her at ease by reassuring her that the answers were confidential and I had heard them all already and I would not be shocked or judgmental about what she told me. It was then I made my big mistake, which was to go further, thinking that a joke might put her at her ease. I smilingly continued: "Unless of course you are going to tell me about

German Shepherd dogs in the bathtub." She paled considerably and gasped, "Oh, God, how could you know that this is my fantasy?" There was a short calming down period for both of us and some abject apologies from me. Then we moved on. I think somehow I may have forgotten to mention this incident to my co-workers. If they learn this information now for the first time, "*mea culpa*."

My favorite experience that still boggles my mind occurred when I asked one couple in their late sixties the routine question of how often they had intercourse. He was a big-boned, red-faced farmer in bib overalls who looked like he would rather be almost anywhere else but in my office. She was thin, had a pleasant face, and rather reminded me of the grandmother on a hillbilly TV program. There was a long pause after I asked the question and I thought they might refuse to answer anything that personal, but it soon became clear that they were just using the time to think about it.

Finally the wife looked at her husband somewhat shyly and said she thought maybe about six or seven times. He hastened to agree, but then added that this was about right, but he wanted me to know that of course they were getting on in years now and slowing down considerably. I still could not code the answer: Was it six or seven times a week, a year, a lifetime? "Oh no," the wife said innocently: "a day of course." These people did not joke; I believed them.

I did wonder why they were in the clinic at all and, what is more, how they had even found the time. Maybe it was I who needed the workshop.

# E.    Never Too Old

This next experience really does not belong in this section. I am not sure where else it fits, but it is so good and I love telling it so I am going to indulge myself. If I need an excuse, it follows the last case in that it says something about the folly of having preconceptions and it deals with a questionnaire.

In the course of some research I was doing, I had to ask subjects more than a hundred possible questions, and by the rules they all had to be asked and all of the responses recorded. One of the sections had to deal with substance usage. I was interviewing what I thought of as a "little old lady." To be more accurate, that meant she was probably about the same age as I am today. I had asked about tobacco and alcohol use and received strong negative replies from her, so when I came to the part about drugs I thought it might be safe to skip that part. I was concerned that these questions might offend her.

On the other hand, the reliability and validity of the research demanded that I ask them and so I continued, "Have you ever used marijuana?" She tucked her head down just a bit so she faced away from me and slyly answered, "Oh, I do a doobie now and again." It was clear she was being honest and I tried not to blink or laugh, but I think she caught my surprise and was amused by it. Never trust your preconceptions. Now that I have reached my own old age, I am so much more aware of just how young, naïve and silly I was back then. The main lesson is clear: You are never too old.

## F.    Not So Gay

In my personal life and practice I have known people who are gay, those who hate gays, and those who defend the rights of consenting adults to do in private whatever pleases them. I belong to this latter group. The more polymorphic forms of sexual behaviors have at times surprised me, but to some extent I have encountered most of them, German Shepherds notwithstanding.

One man came to an initial appointment with his wife. He soon made it understood that he was seething with hatred for all homosexuals. The basis of his anger soon became apparent: his own son was gay and the very thought was intolerable to him. Since the time his son came out at the age of seventeen, the father had neither seen, spoken to or even acknowledged his existence. I had heard of people who had disowned or rejected their children to the point of stating that they were dead to them, but I had never met one. My new patient stated his bias quite bluntly and said he did want to talk about the issue. He said he loved his wife and he was there only because she had threatened to leave him if he did not come to see me.

According to his wife, who at first remained quiet while he ranted, their son was now dying of AIDS and she would not be denied her last moments with him. She intended to go to be by her son who was now in a hospital in another city. Her husband could come with her or stay at home, either way she was going. What was more, if her husband could not find it in his heart to forgive the son, then she could not find it in hers to forgive her husband. He said he would agree to see me privately, and he would go with her, but beyond that he could promise nothing. We only had a week. I squeezed him into my schedule three times.

145

In these sessions he poured out his anguish, confusion and rancor. It would take many more pages to describe the slow, halting progress he made towards even the slightest change. I think what finally brought relaxation of his defenses was when he was able to talk about his son as a child and he got in touch with the happiness and pride this had brought him; and the love. At last he agreed that to go with his wife to the hospital might be possible but that a non-negotiable condition would be that the son's partner never be present when he was there. His wife was invited to attend the last half-hour of the session and she seemed very happy with his willingness to compromise.

After their son died, the wife called to thank me for my help and to tell me what happened. She said there had been a reunion "of sorts" between father and son. Her husband even agreed to attendance by his son's partner and his friends at the funeral, again with the condition that they would not sit near him and his wife or try to speak to them.

As I write this, I know how unsatisfying the conclusion must be to the reader. It was to me. I hope it does not sound trite or facetious, but I wanted to hear of a tearful reunion of the two men, with the father confessing his love for his son while soft music played in the background and swelled to a crescendo as the two embraced, and the son quietly closed his eyes with a smile on his face. Only in the movies. That is the problem with this business; it is real life. The patients get better or they don't; often I never find out what happens to them. They just leave. If I do hear anything, it is like this, a brief phone call: "Everything is okay." Okay; how Okay? I want details. If you need your ego stroked or expect gratitude from most of the patients, look elsewhere; often it is enough to be paid.

As in the following example, of all the problems people have come to see me about, issues involving homosexuality in the patient's family members often cut the deepest, last the longest and are most difficult to resolve. The angriest man I ever had in my office came to complain that his wife had divorced him. He could tolerate the fact that she had left him, but what he could not abide was that she had left him to move in with another woman as lovers. He soon left therapy and I doubt that he ever did get over it. It was clear to both of us that, for reasons he could never face, he needed to hang on to his anger.

I have counseled a number of people while they were going through a divorce or its aftermath. These cases are usually fairly straightforward and often follow a somewhat predictable pattern, similar to those experienced by people who face any loss. Elisabeth Kübler-Ross described these as Denial, Anger, Bargaining, Depression and eventual Acceptance; although not everyone goes through all of these, or in that exact order. This man did not want to be healed.

One of my favorite stories about people exhibiting discomfort with gays occurred when, after some consideration, I introduced a gay man into a mixed-gender, but definitely heterosexual therapy group. He asked that he be allowed to tell the other members that he was gay when he was ready. I agreed. The group was glad to have a new member. One of the men immediately invited him to go fishing, and a woman member "mentioned" that she had a niece who was single. Then Sam dropped the bomb. The two men nearest to him moved their chairs away; the woman glared. Everyone examined the ceiling for a while and no one spoke. Eventually it all worked itself out and he was accepted. Then a short time later I watched a Bob Newhart show on TV which almost completely mirrored the situation and response in our group. What follows what: Art or Life?

## G.   Ted's Story

When I worked in VA hospitals, I heard many reports by female veterans that they had been subjected to sexual harassment and frequently had been raped in the Service. Some were re-victimizations of women who had already been sexually abused in their youth prior to joining the military. To me this made it a doubly awful event. Neither their families nor the nation they volunteered to serve protected them. For what I thought to be good reasons, whenever possible most of these patients were seen by female therapists. In one hospital, group therapy was offered for these women veterans. I had not previously considered the similar abuse of males.

When I began counseling Ted, he was vague about why he had asked for help and at one point I considered telling him that most of what he was talking to me about was not worth the time he was taking. He complained of minor injustices like not making rank as fast as he thought he should and being put on the duty roster too often, or being teased unfairly by other troops. Then one day he stopped and said, "I was raped."

What poured out was a long history of sexual abuse that began in basic training and continued as he was passed from unit to unit, accompanied by a quiet word from his current rapists to the new abusers. This situation persisted throughout his military service and ended only when he developed a medical problem that brought the possibility of his being homosexual to the attention of his commanding officer. Ted was quickly discharged from the military without prejudice and with "good paper." These were not the days of "Don't Ask, Don't Tell." They were the days of

Don't Tell.....Ever; that is if you wanted a military career to continue.

He said that he was not a homosexual and in my opinion he was not. We explored this and I am convinced that he was just a malleable and frightened young man. Once the original rape began, he did not know how to stop it. As with many rape victims, therapy took a long time and it was difficult to convince him that it was not his fault. He refused to report the abuse even now as a civilian and I honored his decision. He said it would be denied and covered up by the military. Having been in the Army myself, I suspected this was true. On the last day when both he and I agreed that he was ready to move on, he asked if he could hug me. Without question I did so. He cried because he said he was afraid no one would ever accept him if they knew what had happened to him. I think to Ted this hug represented my acceptance of him and a promise he would be able to return to a normal life with other men in the future. You already know that in different circumstances I would not have hugged a patient. I think it would border on malpractice not to do so in this circumstance, rather than the other way around. Either way, Ted needed this from me.

# H.   A Good Catholic Man

These two cases deal with relationships so I include them here. They also typify how frequently psychology and religion become intermixed. It was for this reason that I belonged to an interdisciplinary group that include both mental health workers and religious leaders in the community. I referred patients to a minister, imam, priest, or rabbi several times, and they sent members of their flock to see me. In addition, we held periodic discussions of shared cases and of ethical and therapeutic situations.

In the first case, the man I saw on intake was crying and could hardly tell me his story. He was a lifelong Catholic and, against his vehement protests, his wife had divorced him and then subsequently remarried. His concern was that, as he understood the laws of the church, that she was living in sin and would certainly go to hell. He still loved her to some extent and at least had concerns for her as the mother of his children. What now brought things to a crisis was that recently a "Good Christian Woman" and a member of his church had fallen in love with him and was encouraging him marry her, or at the very least to go to bed with her. How could he now compound the sins of his wife by committing adultery himself? He was conflicted and torn by his dilemma.

I asked why they had not brought this problem to their priest. He said he was too embarrassed to discuss sex with a priest and the woman he was seeing thought his concerns were silly. She did not see a reason to bring them to the confessional or to make their relationship known publicly, even to a priest. These issues were way out of my league. One of the priests in our group was a close acquaintance of mine and we sometimes met for coffee. This time I invited him and picked up the bill. He recommended that the man come to see him. I was not told what transpired, but evidently he and his new girlfriend met with Father Mark and the problem was resolved to everyone's satisfaction; including God's I imagined. The man later called to thank me and I was pleased that this had been solved in the appropriate venue.

Another case presented at the interdisciplinary conference pertained to a woman who decided to test her faith, and possibly God's patience, when her boyfriend left her. She knelt praying in the middle of a freeway asking that God bring the boyfriend back or let her die. She almost received the last option. A semi-trailer swerved just enough to knock her to the median where she lay unconscious until she was picked up by an ambulance. She was now on the surgical unit, but the presenting psychiatrist said the patient would shortly be transferred to his unit and he asked for everyone's input. There was a lively discussion and several good suggestions were offered to him. One that drew chuckles from everyone was the terse, "Medicate her." Actually, that seemed to be the best thing to do in the short run. After the meeting, the psychiatrist asked me to see her. I passed on this one until she was stabilized on medication, but she was soon transferred to a private hospital. I lost the opportunity for what probably would have been a fascinating experience. I still wonder what happened to her. For the next few weeks I reviewed the daily paper for possible news of her, but nothing was ever printed.

My private opinion was that a therapist who possessed a similar religious background might have been a better referral. I am uncomfortable when a patient wants to mix too much of their private religious belief system into our therapy sessions. I of course respect their beliefs and the role faith plays in an emotionally healthy person, but too often I am not part of the belief system they express, and I do not know the limits of the overlap.

This brings up an interesting experience: Often at the beginning of a relationship with a patient, I am asked if I am a Christian or perhaps if I belong to a specific sect of religion. Sometimes they ask me this question when they first meet me as a test and as a serious consideration in their acceptance of me as their therapist. I have never answered this question, and yet neither have I ever been rejected as the person's therapist. I respond by asking what their concerns are, then to respect those concerns, and to make clear that I would never belittle their faith or attempt to dissuade them from their practice of religion. That seems to address their real fears and I tell them that if they ever feel that I have crossed this line they are to let me know immediately. I will apologize for anything I might have done to cause distress and avoid repeating my mistake in the future. As we do everything else, we will talk about it. Following this explanation, we are able to begin therapy and there has never been any more discussion of my personal beliefs.

# I.    The Sex Therapist

Irma was not a patient. She was a woman who made an appointment through the receptionist in my private practice to see me on a professional matter. Physicians are used to these types of calls. They are usually made by drug representatives or medical supply salespersons. For a psychologist it was rare to be visited by any outside person and I was curious as to the nature of her visit. When we introduced ourselves, she said her name was Irma and her profession was sex therapy. She had my attention. She explained that she did not possess an advanced academic degree in this specialty, but that she had extensive formal training and held several certificates documenting her expertise. She could provide me with professional references if I required them.

Her proposal was that I consider making referrals to her in whatever cases I thought might be appropriate. She worked with both couples and patients by themselves and assured me that she maintained a discreet office in her home that upon further inquiry consisted mainly of a bed, and that she had adequate facilities and materials for practice sessions or, it seemed, the "tools of the trade." I resisted the impulse to ask what these were. She then suggested several problem areas in which she believed she could be most helpful, and described a few areas of her past successes.

I had many questions. Based on my previous training and experience in this area at the medical school, I must say that she was very knowledgeable and current with relevant literature and recent advances in practice. She approached the topic very professionally as one might any other therapeutic intervention.

It was an intriguing idea when considered independent of any legal or moral questions which, when I thought about it, might be considerable. On the other hand, patients are often given explicit instructions or counseling as to how they might change an unsatisfactory sex life. I have done this myself on occasion. Some clinicians routinely provide literature or recommend what might be considered sex toys. I have not done this, but in rare circumstances I could understand suggesting explicit films to patients for private use. In the clinics I assisted in at the medical school, patients were instructed in new skills as part of the program. As I mentioned above, they were then expected to practice them in their rooms, although the only feedback to the clinicians was verbal. There was never any (dare I say it?) hands-on training.

Irma offered to demonstrate some of her techniques to me at the office she maintained in her home. This as I previously had ascertained seemed to center on a room with a bed. She was sure I would be convinced of the value of her services if I experienced them firsthand. I did not immediately comprehend if this was to be as an observer or a direct participant, but either way I had to decline her services: all of them.

It would be rare that I saw clients who could benefit from such a consult but, in all honesty, I had sometimes known patients for whom a service such as this might have been useful. My overriding concern was how this arrangement might be viewed by the authorities to whom I was dependent for my license and professional memberships. Not to mention my wife. I would assume that Irma also visited some of my colleagues and I wondered if they had accepted her offers: any of them.

# VIII.   THE SCARY ONES

As you already know, not all stories turn out well, and many people cannot or will not change. For some the future already seems to be written in their genes, environment, or both. For those people I have felt sadness but am more often amazed at how much they can accomplish in life despite their limitations. On the other hand, a few patients I saw genuinely frightened me. Fortunately there were not many of these. I have worked on locked psychiatric wards where potentially dangerous and violent people were committed. Usually I felt much safer on those wards than in most bars after midnight or in the streets of some large cities in broad daylight. I observed that, at least in my experience, when a patient attacked someone, it was never one of the housekeeping staff. Those staff and the food service workers, both groups being mostly hard-working and low-paid, seemed to treat the patients with courtesy and respect. The patients responded to this by talking with them in a friendly manner. I think the patients knew that these people were not the enemy. I did my best to emulate the attitudes and behavior of these workers. This assessment may only be a Liberal fantasy of mine and I may be wrong about all of this, but I don't think so.

## A.     Charles Whitman

---

This is obviously not going to be a story about one of my own patients, but I was at the University of Texas on August 1, 1966 when a man named Charles Whitman shot and killed so many people. I include a few details of this shooting because when I mentioned it in a group of students recently, few of them had heard of it, and because it was an important event in my own life. On the fatal day, Whitman went to the observation platform of the university tower 231 feet above the ground armed with a large collection of guns and ammunition, many of them purchased that morning. He proceeded to kill thirteen people and wound thirty-two. Two more subsequently died. An ex-marine marksman, he was able to shoot people from all directions and in some cases five-hundred yards away. He was finally killed when police stormed the tower.

I was waiting to have lunch with a friend and he was late. I was annoyed at the time, but his tardiness quite possibly saved both our lives. We and other students were soon stuck in the building not knowing what was happening outside although we could hear shots being fired. A sniper in full battle dress rushed past us and fired a shot out of an upstairs window. No one explained what was happening because no one really knew. When it all ended, students stumbled outside, talking excitedly, hugging each other. All of us still looked up at the tower apprehensively. It had been a proud and benign symbol of the university, but it was now a reminder of fear and death.

This was the first of the terrible and senseless shootings that have become so common in America. It seems now that each event briefly shocks and outrages, and then far too quickly takes its place in the progression of madness and is repressed and forgotten. I do not think of that day often, but for me, it will never be completely forgotten.

I know that I, and other mental health professionals, wonder if we could have detected the trouble coming if we had seen him in therapy, and, if so, if we could have helped prevent it. Maybe not. Subsequent findings showed he had a brain tumor. At any rate he had gone to the Student Health Center where he complained of severe headaches. He was seen, but never returned for his next scheduled appointment. Unfortunately, in many cases the person does not give us the opportunity to help.

Some good did result from the massacre. Dr. Ira Iscoe successfully campaigned for, in fact demanded, a student counseling center on campus. Mental health staff were added to the Student Health Center as well. It was there that I later worked while on a practicum. On a campus of forty-thousand students, both mental health resources were increasingly well used by students and I think they proved their worth. Similar facilities have become an integral resource on most college campuses. Today there are crisis risk management teams and numerous ad hoc reserves of well-trained personnel who respond to tragedies ranging from school shootings to the 9-11 aftermath. We always seem to wait for bad things to happen before we change the way we do business. We seldom make prepare in advance. Barn doors always shut too late.

## B.    Tick Tock

I was on intake duty when the receptionist asked me to come to the lobby and talk with a boy's parents. Usually so calm and used to handling crises, this time her tone was fearful and urgent. When I came out, I saw there were three people in the far end of the waiting room. The remainder of the room, which was usually crowded, was vacant. The boy in question, Harold, stood nearby while his parents told me in excited whispers that he was experiencing yet another schizophrenic breakdown and needed hospitalization. They stressed that when I saw him I was under no circumstances to mention the watchband he was wearing on his head. I was of course curious but did not see a watchband. Instead, he was wearing a blue wool watch cap on his head in the summer. I called a ward and told the staff to expect an admission. Sometimes campus police backups are called, but they have a dim view of people who call them too often for minor emergencies. I did not want to exceed my quota. I invited Harold to come into my office. Since he was a nineteen-year-old adult, I wanted to interview him alone, unaccompanied by his parents. He sauntered into the interview room, slumped into a chair and looked at me defiantly. He then pulled off the cap and I saw that he indeed had an expansion watchband so tightly wrapped around his forehead that the skin was bleached white beneath it. It was soon clear that he was almost daring me to call attention to it but, heeding the parents' warning, I did not. He seemed to relax slightly. It was rapidly clear that he was experiencing both hallucinations and paranoid delusions. I think he knew he needed help or we would not have gotten this far with him. After a few minutes of talking, he agreed to go to the "Psych Ward." He had been in one before.

I walked Harold to the unit and instructed the staff there not to mention the watchband. They would know what to do and I left to interview the parents. When I again talked to them, they explained that their son believed that aliens were trying to steal his thoughts and replace them with evil messages of their own. He thought the watchband was his only protection from this and only the aliens could see this device. To him anyone who mentioned it was de facto an alien and had to be immediately "neutralized" by him using any means possible. In the past this had generated an onslaught of violence. In his mind he was only doing what was logical to protect himself. As Harold was a husky young man, I was glad I had listened to his parents' advice. Soon after the medications took effect, he removed the watchband but it was documented that he wanted it back when he left the hospital, just in case. Meanwhile the staff examined the watchband and I dropped by to have a look at it. None of us could figure out how he managed to stretch it to go around his head, even though his forehead might have been smaller than ours. I suppose that extreme conditions call for extreme measures.

Over the years I have seen many patients wearing aluminum foil on their heads for similar reasons or to keep out the voices that speak to them. Some wear other items of self-protection or engage in strange rituals. It is like the joke about snapping fingers to keep the elephants away. "But there are no elephants here. See, it works!"

Many homeless people appear to be alcoholics or drug addicts when in fact they are tormented by the symptoms of schizophrenia and they use self-medication or rituals to alleviate their suffering. The sad thing is that they frequently end up in jail rather than receive the mental health assistance they really need. More on this in the next case.

## C.    The Sunrise

Notice that most mental institutions were built in what were at one time the boondocks. They were placed far outside the existing town limits where land was cheap and they were out of sight of the larger community. Now, due to the rampant growth of many areas, they are often surrounded by encroaching urban sprawl. I suppose developers would like to make golf courses on the land or build gated communities. As the patient population decreases, the expense of maintaining these large, sometimes partially vacant, facilities grows. Governments, desperately searching for revenue, have sought to sell these properties. Largely due to the increased use of phenothiazines beginning in the 1950s and the medications developed since then, mental institutions are emptier. Former patients now live on the streets among us in the areas society tried to keep them far away from. The process, by the way, has been referred to as "dumping." Thousands of people, many of whom were institutionalized by years of hospitalization and who had few survival skills, were released. At worst, they were preyed upon by people for the little money they were given and they were resigned to living in SROs (Single Room Occupancies) hastily carved from larger apartments, divided by plywood into multiple units. Community mental health centers were designed to take up the slack, but they could not force people to use them or to continue taking the medications that had freed them from the hospitals in the first place. Many ended up in a jail cell when their symptoms upset the community. Enough preaching.

Enter Clarence. He was a very intelligent man I met when he was a patient on a psychiatric unit. We had brief

160

but interesting conversations during his stays there. He seemed to be very well read and conversant on a variety of topics. When he took his medications, you would have not suspected the disordered mind that was controlled by them. Off his medications, it was a different story. He was discharged from the mental hospital with a three-month supply of anti-psychotic medication and I did not see him again until early one morning when I was on my way to work. This was in Galveston and the sun was beginning to rise over the water. It was quite a glorious sight. I often took the opportunity to delay my arrival at the hospital to spend a few moments enjoying this view. Just then I saw Clarence sitting on a park bench. Thinking it was an egalitarian thing to do I stopped and asked him if he remembered me, how was he doing, and wasn't this a fine day, etc. After a short period of silence on his part, I decided to continue on my way and let him spend the time alone. Happy with myself, I went on to work.

Two months later Clarence was back on the unit. This time he had punched a man on the street because the voices told him the man was a threat to him. With this information, I decided to read his chart. This was something I had not done before because he had never been a patient of mine. There was a long list of similar events going back several years and, even though he was not always physically aggressive, he was often threatening and abusive and sometimes ended up in jail rather than the hospital.

The next time I saw him, he was back on his medications and was considerably calmer. I asked him if he remembered talking to me on the park bench and he replied, yes he did, and that it was a very stupid thing for me to do. He explained that all the time I thought I was making light chatter he was trying to decide if I was an enemy agent that had taken over the body of the person he thought he knew as Doctor Boeringa. The voices were telling him to defend himself from me, but he had not yet made up his mind what to do when I left. I learned a valuable lesson.

# D.  The Stone-Cold Killer?

I have been inside prisons on visits but never worked in them, and certainly never had a convicted killer as a patient, at least none I knew about. And only two, you can next read about those next, said they had killed someone. Even so, I would guess that some of my patients had killed someone at some point in their lives. I just never knew about it. They were not all harmless neurotics or the worried well.

I was doing research on schizophrenia and related disorders with a team at a state mental hospital where we would obtain patient information and collect blood samples for analysis to include in our study. My primary job was to review the charts of possible candidates who fit the criteria for the study, conduct an in-depth interview and make a tentative diagnosis. To narrow our search, we relied heavily on the presumptive diagnosis from the hospital records. Many of our subjects were committed patients who had already been in the hospital for many years. Some of their charts filled many volumes and the information was usually repetitive and it was a boring task, but it fell to me as I was the junior member of the team. Of more interest was the interview process that not only formed a break for me, but it was often the only time anyone had paid much individual attention to the patients. They seemed to enjoy the opportunity to become special for the time being.

There was very little private space available on the wards so they gave me a small dimly lit room at the far end of a long corridor. I had already interviewed four patients one day and was pleased that at least three of them seemed to meet our criteria for inclusion in the study. Everything went well until I met with my next subject. He was a large

163

and hulking man who was diagnosed with a serious enough disorder that he had been in the hospital for fifteen years. I walked him to the interview room, invited him to sit down, and attempted to put him (and me) at ease by asking: "So, why are you here?" He stared at me for a moment as if deciding whether or not to answer and then said clearly, "I have killed people before, you know." I am not sure if it was the tone of his voice or the word "before" with the implication that he might do it again that frightened me the most.

Maybe he was putting me on, maybe not, but his tested IQ level suggested that he was probably not capable of the intellectual ability to play a joke on me. At any rate, my spider instincts were tingling. I was very gentle with him and tried to get him back to his ward as soon as possible. Suddenly the descriptors of "at the end of a long corridor; small and dimly lit private room" all began to assume a special relevance for me. I rushed through the rest of the interview and skipped several questions. I was relieved when he and I were safely back on the locked unit. Sometimes we had a phlebotomist help us with the blood samples, but more often either my physician partner or, less often, I would do this. This time I deferred to my physician counterpart. After all, he was the doctor and that was his area of expertise.

Sam, if you are reading this, I apologize for not telling you at the time. I thought it best that, with this guy, the information not make you nervous and shaky while you were inserting the needle.

# E.  Walking Bird

I had only two people confess to me that they had killed someone outside of war. One was a man who told me that he was involved with several illegal activities and he said he either hung out with or was a member of what sounded to me like a motorcycle gang. He was vague about this however and, for my part, I appreciated not knowing any more than I had to if it was not directly relevant to his therapy. As far as his ever killing someone, he was exceptionally ambiguous and the details he provided sounded as if they were fabricated. He did not elaborate. I told him that as it was a serious matter, I might have to share this information with my colleagues and possibly the police, but he did not seem concerned. I later consulted other professionals about my responsibilities under the law and we mutually decided that there was no proof aside from the limited information he had given me and even that was unclear. In short, I did not believe him. Many patients brag about doing things that might be illegal and if we report each one of them we would drive ourselves and the authorities to distraction. I advised the man that he could repeat his confession to the authorities if that was what he wished to do. He did not.

There are only a few clear instances where the rules do not bend, nor should they. That is when we become aware of child abuse or elder abuse, neglect or victimization. In most states and most professions, it is a legal requirement to report such abuse. I personally think it should also be a moral and ethical requirement. In a very few circumstances, I have given my patients the option of reporting their actions, but I initiated the calls and made sure that the information was disclosed to the proper authorities. I had to assume that if they told me, they must have wanted me to help them deal with it. At the beginning of work together, I outline reporting conditions and I repeat them if there might be eminent harm to themselves or others. The patients already know the outcome when they tell me about a reportable behavior they might be committing. In this case, it was not that he was lying any more than many people I have seen, but many patients feel embarrassed about being in therapy and they build an exaggerated image for me in order to counter what they may perceive as a weakness in accepting help. He did ride a motorcycle and dress in heavy leathers and boots, but he probably was not in a formal gang. And, in my opinion, he was *not* a killer. This was supported by our subsequent discussions.

The reason he had come to see me was because he faced a cultural dilemma. As a Native American, he had been born on a reservation and he always felt torn between his Indian heritage and the white culture he was now living in. He said that he did not know who he really was. When he signed the clinic register for example, he didn't know whether to use his legal name that was on his driver's license and other documents or his Indian name, Walking Bird. I asked him what name he would like me to use and he said Walking Bird and so it was. In future sessions my receptionist also used his Native American name to address him. This seemed to please him greatly.

During weeks of therapy, he told me the history of his past, growing up on the reservation, how he had left it, and in many ways continued to search for his identity. He said that he read books about "the old ways" and had visited different museums that contained Indian artifacts to try to get in touch with his heritage. At the same time, he was pursuing his college education and had a career choice to consider. He was pulled in two directions and could not decide which way to go. I suggested the method of making a list of each and compare them side by side with their strengths and merits in one column and weaknesses and liabilities in the other. He said he had already done this. "Which side won?" He said it was a wash, leaving him more confused than ever. He imagined his probable future life having the same outcome regardless of the path he chose.

Then he was offered a job, a good one he said, "In the White Man's World, but he had to decide now or he would lose it. He chose to take the weekend to think it over; on Monday he would see me with the decision. I somehow felt almost as anxious as he did. My fantasy was that on Monday he would walk in my office either wearing an expensive new suit and a carrying a brief case, or decked out in full Indian regalia complete with head feathers and a tomahawk. I did not know which image I hoped most for him. I scolded myself, "This is not how therapists are supposed to became involved in their patient's lives."

He was uncharacteristically late for his appointment; then came his phone call, "I am going back to the Res to be a Real Indian." He did not know how it would work out, but he knew that maybe his people needed him as much as he needed them. He hoped so. I wished him well and asked if he would let me know how he was doing? "Of course," he said, but of course like so many other people I still wonder about, he never did call again or write me.

I wish you well, Walking Bird, wherever you are.

## F.   Secret Agent Man

We once briefly had a man on a psychiatry unit who was wildly manic when he was admitted. He claimed to be a secret agent. We did not believe him of course; we had heard such things so many times that we hardly listened to his ramblings. The staff only became excited and stopped him when he attempted to crawl through the heating and cooling vents, a method he said he previously used to escape from Russia. That did not prove anything; other patients had tried this before, no matter how we tried to secure the ceiling panels. He also bragged openly and sometimes specifically about things he said he had done. All these stories sounded equally fictitious and preposterous. Even I have watched enough Bond movies to make up similar stories about imagined exploits. Such grandiosity is not uncommon on a psychiatry ward where secret agents are about as common as Elvis Presley reincarnations. We had previously hosted patients who claimed to have been astronauts, avatars, presidents of the world union and aliens.

Imagine then everyone's surprise when two days after he was admitted, a couple of men in grey suits and impressive badges showed up with court-ordered paperwork to take him to "another more secure facility." Thankfully, I had nothing to do with his admission or hospitalization. Any staff who had documented contact with him was debriefed extensively for hours. When I was asked about him, I suddenly remembered that I had been on vacation during his stay and I had never even seen him. No one checked and I didn't know anything anyway.

Compare this to the case of Walking Bird and his telling me that he had killed someone. In many ways, it sometimes really does not matter what I am told; there is often a deeper truth that I and the patient are searching for. In his case, he wanted me to know that he faced extreme choices in his life and that his dilemma was real.

It would be difficult to sort out the lies, half-truths and outright fantasies that I have heard over the years. If even half-true, some things I have heard were lollapaloozas. I have learned not to gasp, laugh or even shake my head. However, they are all some form of communication. Each is told for a purpose, and each is a form of the truth. It is my job to work with the person and figure out where it all fits. Somewhere in the puzzle of hints the patients offer, they are trying to tell me something important. They want me to use this information to enable them to help themselves. Even if I do not hear them the first time, I will eventually "hear" them if they tell me often enough. Many of the stories I hear and the acting-out behaviors have no relevance within the therapy except to provide me with clues. Even so, sometimes I think I receive TMI.[7]

---

[7] *That's "Too Much Information," if you have not heard it before. My sons frequently use this expression with me, and I suspect my daughters-in-law often think it but are too polite or kind to say it out loud.*

# G.   Guns

When I worked for the VA, I led a number of therapy groups. This form of treatment is both cost-effective and a useful method when dealing with similar problems. For many diagnoses, it is probably the best use of time for both patients and staff as it can bring results more quickly within a critical mass of common experiences. It is especially effective with substance abuse, PTSD sufferers, and patients with similar health issues or serious mental illness. You will recall that one group I led consisted of the most difficult patients in our clinic. They were gladly and appreciatively referred from other staff members. I unofficially named them the "Whiners Group."

This story concerns a different group composed of long-term patients. Most of them had experienced revolving-door hospitalizations for psychosis; however they were now well maintained by assorted medications. Such groups usually have a long history. They roll along from year to year with regularity and provide both ongoing monitoring by the staff and a social peer group for their members. Successive waves of students or staff members generally lead these groups before they move on to their next job or rotation and leave them in an orderly transfer to the next person in line. For instance, I inherited this group from a psychologist who left to take a job somewhere else. I was glad to have responsibility for the group and I looked forward to meeting with them every week. I liked the members and appreciated hearing about their struggles and successes. They were good people who were dealing with the problems life had presented them in the best way they knew.

The group met routinely following lunch. On this specific occasion, I was in the parking lot on my way to go eat with a few of my fellow workers. One of the group members called to me, asking me to come over to where he was standing some distance away. I told my friends to go on; I would catch up with them. He was standing next to his car and when approached he suddenly opened the front passenger door and pulled out a paper bag. Swiftly he opened it and pulled out a gun. My heart stopped, literally I think. It looked like the biggest gun I had ever seen in my life. It loomed in front of my eyes like a cannon. It was a .45 and it was pretty big alright and getting bigger all the time. Was he going to kill me? Himself? The whole clinic? No, he had been feeling suicidal and he wanted to give me the gun for safekeeping. When my legs stopped shaking, I thanked him for his forethought. Quickly, I gently took from him the weapon and the bag of bullets that went with it. We returned to the clinic office where I had him sign an agreement that the gun and bullets would be returned only at my discretion. The armaments were then placed in the safe. I told him he had done a very good thing and I that I would see him shortly in the group session. I decided to skip lunch, go off by myself and contemplate how good life was.

I have not had to deal with many gun-toting patients in my twenty-five years of clinical practice. Those I have, you will read about here. They are not experiences I have easily forgotten.

# IX.    THE SAD ONES

The stories in this section are about children. They stand alone because they are special and I could not put them in any other category. At times they still haunt and sadden me. A friend of mine began work on a children's cancer unit and had to quit. Every time he saw a child, he could only think of his own children and their vulnerability to illness and death. He could not stand to deal with the continued trauma of each day. After a short while, I began to see what he meant. I did not yet have children of my own, but these sick children began to become "mine" and I could not bear to see, for some of them, a continued slide into death. Please understand, there were of course many who improved, regained their health and went home happy, but my emotional balance had been tipped. I too needed to leave. I admire the professionals on the unit who have the love and courage to stay. No matter what their strength, I still know the toll they must pay. I do not think that anyone can remain emotionally untouched by children facing serious illness.

## A.    The Wild Boy

Given the stupidity and cruelty of some parents and the criminally blind eye of society, we continue to have too many cases of poorly nurtured, starving and discarded children. In cases of children who fail to gain weight, we even have a term for it: failure to thrive. I think it should be used to refer to all forms and stages of severely arrested development. Through neglect and through natural causes, critical stages of development may pass and the child may never obtain crucial skills, including socialization and even speech. This was the case in a nine-year-old boy brought to the facility by a child-find program.

Juan was rescued from a locked horse stable where he had been fed by having food shoved under the door. He had very little human contact. I think that he was close to what is referred to as a Feral Child, although in the strictest interpretation this would have meant that he had experienced almost no human contact while growing up. Throughout history there have been stories of human children raised by animals, and not just fiction like Romulus and Remus, the founders of Rome, or Mowgli in Kipling's *Jungle Tales*. Medical literature contains some examples of children who have been raised in extreme conditions with only minimal nurturance. In this specific case, the animals were humans. Juan's father was a crude, cruel man who had a ranch far from town. He brought a simple-minded, young woman there to cook, clean up and care for his more basic needs, as he saw them. Their child was an inconvenience.

Juan was very cute and he quickly won the hearts of all the staff when he was brought to a children's hospital where I did part-time consulting. He had dark brown eyes and with adequate nourishment his face grew more chubby and he became more active. His mental age was probably about four or five. However, because most of the usual measurements and milestones were not present, it was difficult to evaluate him with any certainty. As one example, he had only rudimentary speech. He also lacked other abilities that someone his age should have developed. He possessed only the most primitive social skills. I had had no training or experience in dealing with any situation like his and all I could do was to observe him and record what I saw. I could not even administer an IQ test because he was unscorable even at the lowest levels. Developmental tests had been attempted, but Juan either did not cooperate sufficiently or the base rates were not observed. This was not my area of expertise and I did not know of any mental health professionals in the vicinity who specialized in the special needs of someone like Juan. He certainly needed more intensive psychological and emotional care than I was able to provide, but we wanted to wait until his medical status was stabilized before considering the next stage of treatment and placement. Also the legal rights and status of the parents needed to be resolved.

One asset Juan did have, despite his dreadful early experiences, was a winning smile and this, combined with his dark hair and bright eyes, easily attracted people to him. Considering his impoverished background, it seemed that everyone who met him somehow wanted to make it all up for him. Despite admonishments to remain careful around him, it was hard for the staff not to believe that if only he had more love and maybe a few extra hugs, he would respond and grow to his full potential. Because of this, a strict protocol was established that outlined the behaviors to be followed in his care. One of the rules was to not to pick him up unless it was necessary and then to be careful when holding him because if he felt uncomfortable for any reason, he would suddenly lash out violently.

One childcare aide thought these precautions were silly and she would often cuddle him when she thought she was not being observed, and she sometimes gave him forbidden treats. With these reinforcements, Juan naturally sought her out and this in turn increased her affection for him. She announced to her co-workers that she wanted to adopt him and no amount of reasoning would dissuade her from her plan. One day, again in violation of the guidelines, she picked him up and evidently squeezed him a little too tightly; in response, he bit a piece of flesh out of her shoulder.

This persuaded Administration that we were neither able to provide adequate evaluation or training for him, nor to keep the staff safe from harm. We were forced to immediately transfer him to a larger, more secure and experienced medical facility. I was unable to follow his history and never saw nor heard about him again. I often wonder what became of him. Don't you?

## B.    Carole Lee

Soon after the wild boy left, a bitter-sweet tale began for the staff and me when social workers brought a young girl to us. She too had suffered from neglect but not nearly as severely as he had. Fortunately, this case allowed us to do some good and ended more happily. I think it helped us all to heal from the loss of Juan. Eleven-year-old Carole Lee arrived dirty and smelling, wearing only a T-shirt, dirty panties and a pair of ragged jeans. No other clothing accompanied her. Her feet were brown and calloused as if she had never worn shoes. We knew for certain that she had never gone to school. The only reason she came to the attention of authorities was because a neighbor had reported her family to a local child protection agency.

I did not meet Carole Lee's parents because they lived a long distance from the hospital and, as they were literally dirt poor, they could not afford to travel. Usually one condition for accepting a child was that the parents visit on a regular basis; however, in this case we made an exception. It is a harsh judgment to make, but the term we most frequently heard describing her parents was "ignorant." I think this was true in an objective sense in that they were essentially uneducated and had little exposure to the world outside their small farming community and they had little interest in expanding it.

According to a social work report, the parents were not especially mean or neglectful, but they had too many children to look after and minimal resources. Two babies were born after Carol Lee and they quickly displaced her in their parents' attention.

Her T-shirt was clumsily hand-lettered with "I'm Stupid," which brought an immediate angry response from everyone who saw it, including me. Not surprisingly, this shirt was quickly lost in the laundry and never seen again. Over the next week, the staff brought in a flood of feminine clothing outgrown by their own daughters as well as many new items, some with the tags still on them. As they say in Texas, "She cleaned up real well." She was a pretty child to begin with, but with all of the attention and her new outfits, she positively glowed.

I saw her for at least an hour-long session each day that I was at the hospital and she was like a flower blossoming. She reached out to new concepts and grew more confident and social. Her teachers reported how much she enjoyed learning new things and in their description used the analogy of a sponge. As I have said, child psychology is not my forte, but my opinion was that there was nothing emotionally or developmentally wrong with Carole Lee. Certainly she was not "stupid." The various test instruments administered supported this fully even without making many allowances for her limited background.

Of course eventually she had to return to her family. I do not know what happened then. The follow-up care was accomplished locally and by then my contract at the hospital had ended and I was busy starting new employment. This did not mean that I had forgotten her. I hope that today she is a happy, secure mother raising children every bit as wonderful as I think she was. And that none of them will ever wear a demeaning T-shirt.

I cannot repeat too often how, in spite of the many rewards my profession has brought me, there is always the frustration that, after being such an intense part of the lives of patients, they have vanished from my radar never to be seen or heard of again. In this case, I was concerned not only about Carole Lee but also the other children in the family and the parents. Multiply these by all the people I have counseled and it is obviously impossible to keep up with them all. I hope this does not make me uncaring or callous, just realistic. Here in this book I honor a few.

## C.    The Three Graces

During my internship I had a rotation on a cancer ward for children. I noticed that there were three preteen girls who had bonded together on the ward. This created a good opportunity for group work so I began holding sessions with them. It started out very low key; I knew it would be unwise to push them. If I did, they would probably withdraw into that silent world in which adults are not welcome. So we talked about general subjects and I let them chose the topics. Sometimes they would mention some aspect of their medical regimen but, for the most part, I think it was just the normal run of girl talk that any girls their age might indulge in. At least I thought so. What did I know about what they or any other pre-adolescent girls talked about or felt? Sometimes I was just a fly on the wall, asking for clarification at times or making a very mild and tentative interpretation but mostly just glad they had let me into their thoughts at all.

Then one day they asked if they could bring their drawings and of course I was pleased. So far the sessions had remained at a fairly surface level and art is often a language that speaks of deeper underlying thoughts and feelings. It was clear that they had discussed this among themselves beforehand because they brought a number of large books of drawing paper with them. I was the one who was not prepared for what they wanted to share.

With the drawing pads, they brought numerous cuttings from fashion magazines and their own renderings of dresses in which they would like to be buried. I sat there stunned and close to tears. They animatedly discussed the pros and cons of each dress, the funeral arrangements, and who they wanted to attend. In different circumstances they could have been selecting wedding dresses and choosing maids of honor. If they noticed how profoundly moved, withdrawn and unusually silent I was, they did not comment on it. They were, of course, dealing with their own death and in a way that I could not have predicted. This was after all what I had set out to help them do, was it not? Yet now that I had the tiger by the tail, I did not know what to do with it. I had wanted an open discussion but now that it had begun, I didn't know what might be "therapeutic" in these circumstances or how to proceed. I did the safest thing: I did nothing. It was then that I realized that I had few skills and no language for working with anyone at this level of sadness, much less children. The fault was mine and I accepted it. At my very core, I had not yet begun to face my own mortality. How could I face theirs?

I continued with the group until I rotated to another assignment. I think I helped them a little, maybe, probably not too much. My primary assistance was possibly to give them more time to talk together and my approval and support for what they were doing. I certainly learned a great deal from the experience and benefited from confronting my own fears and emotions.

# D.   Ronny

My inner struggle with my own mortality coincided with seeing one of my patients die in another hospital, and my emotional response to "The Three Graces" facing death. This was reinforced by the situation facing so many other patients on this same children's ward. It was such a private time for both the patients and their families that I never wanted to intrude. I hoped instead to make myself available and to be invited in to work with them. In this case, however, the staff asked me to talk to one of the parents.

May was a single mother who was near exhaustion with the burden of her child's illness and her concern about the extended absence from her job it necessitated. She spent all her time with her son Ronny, who had a particularly virulent and nasty form of cancer. Although it was being treated aggressively, it continued to grow and increasingly threatened the boy's life. The staff said that no matter what time of day, she was at his side. I met her and her son Ronny and after a while she acknowledged that she needed some respite, but she could not bring herself to leave because he might need her while she was gone. She said he cried each time she left him, even to go the restroom. Translated: What if he dies and I am not there to comfort him? I did not ask her about the father. The stress of a child's serious illness often destroys families.

I bonded easily with Ronny and, since the mother observed how the boy gradually accepted me, she would leave to get a snack in the canteen or go home for a few hours. The reason he was so comfortable with me of course was because I was the only care provider not wearing a white uniform, and the only one who did not "do something" to him each time they came in the room. He was deeply conditioned to associating a white uniform with impending pain. I only brought smiles. Each time she left, I had to promise his mother that either I or a staff member would call her if there was any change in his condition.

This boy was very likeable as he smiled easily and enjoyed talking about a large variety of his interests. He asked questions about my life and activities as well. "Did I have any children?" "No not yet." "Would I like to have some?" "Yes, some day." "A boy or a girl?" "One of each." "What would the boy be like?" "Just like you, I hope." "Giggles." I looked forward to the time I was able to spend with him on the ward and even had fantasies about possibly continuing the relationship when (if) he got out of the hospital. I guess I always knew this was a long shot, but I was not prepared for what happened next.

After being away for a weekend, I unthinkingly walked into Ronny's room. He was gone. The bed had been made and his possessions were missing. I knew instantly what this meant. He had not been transferred to another room, he had died. It was a shock to me and I stood there in the empty room for a long moment, but I repressed my immediate feelings and went on almost as if nothing had happened. We call that denial. After that I learned what the rest of the staff already knew, which was to attend the morning meetings or to check the roster each day before entering a patient's room. I eventually talked with May. She did not ask for any assistance or follow-up and so, as I thought, the matter ended there. I had other patients to see.

All was well until a month later. I was in a shopping mall and a small boy with blond hair was walking ahead of me. When he reached a point where sunlight made his entire scalp seem bald, I immediately flashed back to my patient Ronny. Suddenly, uncontrollably, I stood and bawled. Slowly I found my way through the tears to the side of the hallway and out of the way of curious traffic. I knew then why the colleague with small children said he could not work on that unit. Neither could I. I did not abandon current cases, but when I said goodbye to the last patient, I did not request a second rotation there. I am glad there are professionals who have the strength and love to help these children. I find I become too emotionally overwhelmed and even though there are wonderful successes, I could not stand even the occasional losses.

# E.   The Dream Girl

I feel the need to write these stories together with the happier, sometimes even funny ones, but it is not an easy task. Writing about the patients has brought their memories back in an all-too-sharp focus, and has reopened the pain I felt at the time. I include them in this book because I need to be honest with myself. And because I think they may be helpful to the reader. I do not mean to be maudlin when I say these people are still with me.

Much of my career has been spent in VA hospitals working with adults so I found it a refreshing change to do some "moonlighting" from my day job and spend time with children and adolescents. In one facility for teen-age patients, a girl made a serious suicide attempt and was consequently committed as an in-patient. The director asked me if I would see Lily on a pro bono basis; that meant seeing her without fee as a public service. This is a common practice in many professions and is a way of giving back to the community and being able to help those who otherwise would not be able to pay for our services.

She was open to therapy and I quickly found that I enjoyed the time we spent together. She was a very bright and insightful person. During the course of my trying to understand and help her, she mentioned that she sometimes had vivid dreams and I seized on this as a means of communication. I asked her to tell me about these dreams and when she said she was aware of them but unable to recall them, I asked her to instead close her eyes and envision stories. She had a very rich imagination and was soon immersed in a world different from the one in which she had felt a great deal of pain, suffering and rejection. My plan was to help her merge this world with the one of reality. I hoped this would allow her to develop coping skills, and perhaps better survive in the real world. Her stories were truly poetic and I felt this girl had wonderful potential if only she were able to reach it and surpass her admittedly terrible environment. It is not good to become emotionally involved with one's patients, but I admit that my delight with her and her rapid progress sometimes caused me to slip over the line. Not too far, but I began to imagine this bright new world for her. I knew her ability, and I wanted badly for her to be able to reach her potential.

Then a representative from the insurance company called. Clearly following some review formula, it was noted that in two sessions I had not documented the current suicide potential in my notes. "Is this still a problem?" "Since she was admitted for attempted suicide, perhaps this is no longer a threat?" "When can she be discharged?" I did consider her to still be a viable risk for suicide and I regretted my oversight in not indicating this more explicitly in my chart notes. I forgot that we were not dealing with a human being here, but instead, on the part of the company, only tables of risk assessment and cost containment. In my next notes I carefully delineated the extent of the risk in striking terms to ensure that the insurance company could expect a serious lawsuit if she were denied treatment and as a result harmed herself in any manner.

Another week's coverage was automatically granted, but I could not stave off the inevitable. Inexplicably, the insurance paid hundreds of dollars a day for inpatient care but nothing if I was to provide outpatient care at a ridiculously lower rate. I was of course willing to see her pro bono in my private practice if necessary. Even this option became moot before the end of the week. I arrived for our scheduled session two days later and found that the family had moved out of the state. Lily had to go with them of course and was discharged. She was already on her way to her new home.

Six months later I was given the news that Lily had killed herself. There was only minimal information beyond this except that she never received therapy in the new location. Case closed.

# X. DEALING WITH DEATH

Few people spend much time contemplating their own death. In a small group focused on death and dying, I once asked participants to lie on the floor and imagine they had died. Most of them admitted that it was too difficult to even contemplate. I remember being in a group when I was first asked to do this so I think I knew how they felt. At fifty I realized that I certainly had lived at least one-half of my life. At seventy-plus now, I am acutely aware of how fast the last twenty years have passed and the probability that in another twenty I will have fallen off the twig. Sobering. Early on I was a great follower of the works of Elizabeth Kübler-Ross. I read her books and attended some of her lectures. I met her once and we discussed her thoughts on death and dying. I have worked on oncology units with both sick and dying adults and, as you know, children. It put me in closer touch with my own mortality: There but for...go I, and all that. What really brought awareness home was attending autopsies. Nursing students were required to observe one as part of their training and several students were sufficiently disturbed that I was asked to help them process the experience. That meant I had to watch one too, didn't it? The first one was as difficult for me as for them. In fact, I think some of the students helped me through it rather than me help them. Strange isn't it, we seldom pall at seeing animals butchered or rows of bloody meat neatly wrapped in cellophane in stores, but we are overcome by seeing a human being cut in an operation or dead.

During morning medical rounds on an oncology ward, a resident was giving his report. He related that on the previous night he had been called from his meal in the downstairs cafeteria to pronounce a patient who had just died. While he was filling out the paperwork, the "dead man" stirred, fluttered his eyes for a moment and said, "Fooled you, didn't I, Doc?" The man went on to describe the sensation, now well publicized, of going down a tunnel towards a bright light and being told he had to go back. This was about the time that Raymond Moody wrote a book about near death experiences called *Life after Life*[8], but it was clear that this very sick man had never read it nor had the resident. The man also described being out of his body and, while floating around, seeing the resident eat his meal. Senior staff in the conference room quickly dismissed the incident and abruptly cautioned their junior that he was there to report on medical facts not science fiction. I later talked to this resident; he had not heard of or encountered the phenomena before and neither had I. This made a great impression on me and even though I never witnessed it, it changed my thinking about death, as it did his.

I have worked on hospital units with severely ill patients and in nursing home units with very old and sometimes very sick patients. In all my cases there is a natural sense of intimacy with the patient, but it is seldom as deep as with these people. The reason may seem obvious: It is often a situation of life or death. I think in the face of death many of the previous secrets and concerns in their life melted into insignificance. The patients could be more open. They could share their fears, their feelings and their joys more easily. A bond like this with any person is a privilege,

---

[8] Raymond Moody, *Life after Life: The Investigation of a Phenomenon—Survival of Bodily Death* (New York: Bantam Books, 1975).

but it is especially so when the stakes are so high. Unfortunately what I had to offer sometimes felt like so little.

## A.    The Red Truck

As a psychologist on consult to medical service, I received all kinds of interesting calls, some of which are described in other parts of this book. One common request was to deal with the difficult, demanding or frightened hospitalized patient who frequently used the emergency call button for minor issues. This drew heavily on staff time. My consistent recommendation was for staff to tell the patient that they would schedule a brief time with him or her at specific intervals. But, staff argued, they didn't have time to do this; they had other duties and patients to take care of. Then I asked them to add up how much time it took each day to run to every call and fluff a pillow, or tell the patient when their doctor would see them, or do the multitude of other minor tasks and most often the non-medical tasks that the most demanding patients were requesting. Usually they would then agree that a fifteen-minute "appointment" with the patient in the morning and afternoon made sense. This way the patients still received the attention they seemed to need, but the staff gained time. Usually this worked.

One man was refusing heart surgery at the last moment. I was called by staff in a panic because the operating room was being held and an entire team was scrubbed and waiting for him. I greeted him in a leisurely manner and sat down with him by his bedside. We talked a little about how things were going when he soon asked me, "I suppose you've come about the surgery, haven't you?" I admitted that was the reason and then just waited. "Well, I knew they were upset, but I didn't think they would call the shrinks in on me." I laughed; he laughed. The patient then told me that the surgeon had never come by to see him. He was not going to let anyone who he had not "looked in the eye" cut him open. After all, it might be the last person he ever saw! I laughed again and said I would call Dr. X and pass this information on to him. The surgeon broke scrub to see him and ten minutes later both were off to the operation. Sometimes success is simple: It just requires listening.

My favorite consult was with a man the nurses suspected of being senile because, according to the written consult I received, he was found several times in the bathroom talking to a mirror about a truck. I spent a little time getting to know him and then asked him if he had anything he wanted to talk about. Almost immediately he began to express concern about this truck of his. He described it as a red truck and one he owned for many years. He loved that truck and it had served him well, but now it was old and rusted and it didn't run so well anymore; he was not sure it could be fixed. What would happen to it now?

It soon became apparent that while he was deeply concerned about his illness and impending death, he could not bring himself to address these issues directly. He was projecting his concerns about himself on that truck. We continued our talk using the metaphor of the truck to discuss what might happen in the future and to sum up all the good things that he had enjoyed in his life. He understood that perhaps it was now time to face what the near future might bring. He said he was ready. The last thing I did was to walk him to the mirror and ask what he saw. He said he saw a sick, old man, but he thought he was going to be okay now.

Psychology is sometimes pretty simple. It is often what is referred to as common sense and, as much as anything else, it is about listening. Too often we think that we have to DO something. This creates an urgency that blocks us from hearing what the other person wants to do, but might be looking for permission or encouragement to do. Listening is not always as easy as it was in the case of the patient with the red truck, but it follows the rule of first doing no harm and it is usually worth the effort.

## B.    The Grave Problem

A physician in the clinic referred a young man to see me because in the course of a physical examination she felt that the man was probably depressed. He was, but his depression was based on specific events in his life. It was what we call a reactive depression. Several years earlier his girlfriend and he were engaged to be married, but she suddenly and tragically died. He could not face going to her funeral or even to remain in the same town with his memories of where they had planned to live together. He quit his job and moved some two hundred miles away. Now, three years later he still thought of her "constantly" and he regretted that he had never said goodbye to her. He felt that he had abandoned her and he experienced tremendous guilt over this. He did not even know where she was buried. Over several weeks of talking with me and trying to work out his feelings, he finally realized that he could never rest until he visited her grave. This had been one of my initial thoughts, but I believed it was necessary for him to determine this action for himself and I was glad that he had done so.

He did not know how he would respond to this visit, and he was afraid to go, but determined to follow through on his plan. In the week before he left, I asked him to imagine obtaining the information he would need, making the trip, going to the grave, and what he might do there that would help to resolve his feelings. He planned to take flowers and hold a private memorial in which he would speak to her of his love for her and ask her forgiveness. I encouraged him to fantasize how he might feel afterwards, specifically how on the trip back, as the miles between them receded, so might his guilt and his attachment to a memory. He was to imagine his change in feelings, never totally forgetting her but moving on to a life with the possibility of new loves and happiness. You might recognize that these are the same kind of suggestions that are often used in hypnotherapy. In this case they created an expectation that was natural to the situation and then reinforced it. He was encouraged to connect the receding miles with diminished feelings of guilt. He came to my office on the Thursday before he left just to say goodbye and for me to wish him luck. He was still a little apprehensive, but he resolved to go and to find some closure.

I would like to say that an instant cure was effected by his confrontation with multiple issues, but when he returned, he stopped by to see me for only a very brief visit. All he would say was that he was glad he had made the trip and he would not need to see me anymore. Of course I left the door open for future contact, but I never heard from him again.

I asked the physician about him, and I was told that she no longer had his medical records; they had been transferred, but she did not know the destination. Once again I was left with feelings that were almost as unresolved as his had been. He had evidently found some closure; why was I to be denied mine? After all the effort on my part to help him and the time we had spent together, I felt somehow cheated. It was like reaching the end of a long book and finding that the last few pages were ripped out and missing.

Then again if what I really wanted was to be told what a wonderful therapist I was, I am still waiting. This desired recognition and praise does not occur often in my profession.

## C.   The Man Who Raised Me

Please do not take the title too literally. The title refers to Bill, the man who was Grand Master of the Masonic Lodge I belonged to. In the process of initiation, he was the one who offered me the final symbolic gesture of acceptance. From a lower position, he took me by the hand and held me up. He raised me. I had tremendous respect for him as a person. He was one of the surrogate fathers I have collected during my lifetime. Some of them, like my uncles, coexisted with my own father while he was still alive. Others over the years filled some specific aspects of the role of a father for me. All of them were deeply loved in some way. When Bill was diagnosed with cancer, he asked me to help him.

I set aside any rule of dual relationships that may have pertained and consented. What is more, I visited him at his home. As I shall argue for a few others' cases: This was not therapy I offered but the help of one person to another. They did not need to be "fixed" and if they asked me to be with them as a friend, not in my professional role, I did not refuse. We had long talks together. In some of them, I learned what it was to always do the right thing and to be an honorable man. One of the many things he shared with me was his personal history. He was proud of his accomplishments and he equally discussed his shortcomings, and his desire to do better, and his regret that he had not always done so. It was never mentioned, but I realized that he knew he had little time left. He was preparing to die in the same manner as he had always faced life: head on and with complete honesty.

When he was finally admitted to a hospice facility, I visited him. During what was to be our last visit together, before I entered his room, the staff confided to me that it was "just a matter of time." Working in several similar places, I have learned to trust the staff. Over the years they know the signs; they can often predict impending death with a very consistent degree of accuracy. I did not know if he even recognized me by then. His eyes were open but seemed glazed, and his breathing was labored. I held his hand and just talked to him. I talked about how he had been a good husband and father, and how he had guided so many people like me in the Lodge over the years. I talked about how proud I had been to know him and how he had touched my life. Finally, I told him that I knew he was tired and his labors were complete; if he felt ready, he could let go, secure in the knowledge that he deserved to lay down his tools and rest. The words may have been for him, but they comforted me as well. Then, still grasping his hand, I bent down and kissed him on the forehead before I left. I did not live far away and when I walked into my house, the phone was ringing. He had passed. I wonder today if he died while I was still in the parking lot, and if I should have waited with him a little longer so that he would not have been alone at the end. Perhaps he was not.

Now obviously in the strictest sense, this man was not a patient, but I appreciate the opportunity to honor him in print. I am pleased to include his story here.

# D.   Coping with Suicides

I do not wish to dwell too heavily on patients for whom suicide intervention was successful. I have never been sure how close they were at the time to actually taking their life when they came to me for help. I have little personal experience but I read that a large proportion of those who fail in their first attempt are glad they survived and they never try again. I wonder if those I could not save might have had happier lives today if they had survived. This is one of the hopes I held out to people who seemed to be wavering.

You never know. One patient came to me threatening suicide. After some time in therapy, I was sure that he had pulled back from the brink. I believed he was well on the way to dealing with the issues in his life. Each time we were together I specifically asked about his overall condition and the possibility of suicide. He always told me that this risk was behind him. At the end of a session on a Friday afternoon, he spent ten minutes working out the timing of our next three appointments. He seemed to look forward to watching some sporting event on TV over the weekend. When he left the office, he made some joke with another patient he knew. I felt certain in my mind that I would see him next Wednesday at 10:00 a.m.

Early Saturday morning his father called to say his son had shot himself. He was in intensive care and not expected to live. I asked permission to go see him and the father agreed. Standing by my patient's bedside, I had several mixed emotions, most of which you can probably imagine. The strongest was anger at him for not giving himself, or me, a better chance. He died later that day.

197

Another suicide was that of a firefighter who months before had worked a blaze where several children burned to death. This was no fault of his; they died before the alarm was called, but it still haunted him. I knew a friend in his company who sent him to me for help. The friend told me that the firefighter's colleagues were supporting him and also monitoring his behavior on and off the job for any signs of possible suicide. I saw him for a month and encouraged him to call me if he ever needed to talk more or ever considered taking his own life. Each time he reached into his shirt pocket and pulled out a piece of paper: "Don't worry, Doc, I've got your number right here." He seemed to be improving and the last time I saw him he again assured me that he would "never do anything that stupid."

He was found dead with a bottle of whiskey by his side and a gun that he had hidden from everyone was still in his hand.

In both cases I faced a dilemma of whether to attend the funerals. After all, I was not a relative and there was even the chance that the families and friends would be angry at my presence. After all, I had failed to save their loved one. They might even sue me. When I did attend both funerals, it was out of respect for the deceased and their families. In addition, I needed closure as much as many of the other people who knew them. Both families welcomed me; they seemed to appreciate my concern. It was healing for me as well.

## E.    A Suicide Pact

Being a teenager is tough. Maybe it has always been so, but I think it is more difficult today for all the reasons that easily come to our minds. I know too that I frequently read or hear about kids making pacts together to try dope, lose their virginity, get pregnant, and even kill themselves. One group of girls in a town not very far from where I once lived decided to commit suicide. Several of the girls made gestures, but thankfully none of the actions were too serious and eventually one of the girls told her parents about the plan. As can be imagined, the whole town was in an uproar, fueled as usual by the "if it bleeds it leads" media. It was decided that all of the girls must receive *post facto* therapy. Several therapists, including me, volunteered to do this on a community service basis. When my patient was put on the schedule to see me, all I knew about the case was what I had read in the papers. Not much.

Lisa, the thirteen-year-old young lady I saw, started off by slouching in her chair and aggressively saying that she didn't know what the big deal was about anyway, and she didn't know why she had to come here. After that brief introduction, she just sulked and mumbled "dunno" to all my questions. Eventually, just to get me off her case as she phrased it, she said that there had been a big football game on Saturday night and they all agreed that they would feign illnesses and stay home. While everyone was away they would kill themselves. No reason was volunteered. She did admit that basically her life was okay except, of course, she could not go to the mall as often as she liked and her parents made her keep a curfew. She seemed to think these were good reasons to be angry at her parents and to kill herself. "They'll be sorry" seemed to be the unspoken "reason," such as it was.

On the designated evening, she pretended that she was sick and would not be going with her family to the game. After several excited phone calls between her friends and herself in which each of them assured the other that they were ready to go ahead with the plan, she set herself to do the deed. Following some ideas that they had read about or seen on TV, she picked up a razor blade. After numbing her wrist with ice cubes she made several superficial cuts. She stopped because "it hurt." Some of the girls thought that sitting in a tub was a good idea, but she did not want to get her dress wet, and she certainly did not want anyone to see her naked. For the next week she wore long sleeve blouses to hide the wounds. Otherwise it was life as usual, "until that stupid Mandy girl blabbed to her parents about it."

If the preceding information seems extremely thin and unsatisfying to the reader, it was no less so to me. This was about all the information I was able to obtain from her. I understood that my colleagues were not getting much more cooperation from their patients. At least in my case, the extent of the parent's involvement seemed to be dropping their daughter off at my office and picking her up. They gave me the impression that they saw it all as one of those silly things teenagers do and they did not think it was very important. They, like their daughter, did not see why all the fuss was made. If they were mad at anyone, it was the newspapers that had "blown it all out of proportion."

Lisa quit coming after the second session. I had no idea then nor do I know now why she and the others planned or attempted a group suicide. Nor do I have any idea how to prevent this from happening in the future. None. I suppose all of us therapists might have joined forces and tried to figure out something better to do, but we didn't, and I don't think it would have helped. As I write this, I still feel the frustration.

# XI.    THE ONES I LOVED MOST

These are, for me, the best stories because they are about people I came to love in a special way. I still care about them. Placing them right after the sadder or more troubling cases was not an accident but an antidote. For those who have already died, I can offer no better memorial than my joy at having known them and my sadness at their passing. If they were still alive, I would like to tell them personally what they meant to me. To write about them instead is like the best of times and the worst of times. I am flooded with the good memories and I am concerned that I will not honor them to the degree that I wish to do. While writing these stories, I have both laughed and shed tears. Both emotions were good therapy for me.

I have called the first three people and the last person in this section by their real names. If I had been able to ask them, I do not believe they would have minded. I think that to not use the names I knew them by would rob them of some of the special love and respect I felt for them. They deserve to be known and acknowledged. I loved them the best and still do.

# A.  Cinderella

Nell was a patient I knew for over fifteen years and during this time she even attended my wedding as an honored guest. I do not remember exactly, but I think that when I first met her she was already at least seventy years old. In reality, she was timeless. In the first therapy session, she walked into my office and was already talking before she even sat down. She knew what she needed to do and how she was going to do it and she was here in order to change her life. Her approach did not change in subsequent sessions. She planned each session and perhaps even rehearsed what she was going to tell me; it often sounded that way. She always started talking as she walked in the door and at exactly the end of the hour she stopped, almost in mid-sentence, got up and left. She then picked up next time just where she had let off, almost as if the past week had been but a pause in the conversation.

She had been adopted into a family with two birth daughters who were older than she and the treatment she received both by them and the stepmother made me think of Cinderella. At one point I gave her the book *The Uses of Enchantment*[9] by Bruno Bettelheim. The story of Cinderella would be a continuing metaphor for our work together. Years later one Christmas she sent me a gift: a Walt Disney porcelain statuette of Cinderella. I displayed it prominently in each of my subsequent offices as a reminder that people can change their lives. When I was discouraged, it gave me

---

[9] Bruno Bettelheim, *The Uses of Enchantment: The Meaning and Importance of Fairy Tales* (New York: Alfred A. Knopf, Inc., 1976).

hope that not everything I did was in vain and some patients did improve even in spite of me.

Soon after my wife and I married, we moved to another state, but Nell continued to send me annual letters recounting her successes. One included her happiness at joining a social group and having been "invited to the dance." Eventually I returned to live in Houston and, when I went to visit her at her home, I took my sons with to meet her. When she was later hospitalized, I visited her at her bedside. Sadly, I was not informed of her death and did not have the chance to say my last goodbyes to her. I regret that.

Nell never asked more of me than to do my job, and my role as she saw it was as a listener, coach and cheerleader. It was clear from the beginning whose responsibility it was to implement change and who was doing all of the work. She was. The details of therapy are incidental and would add but little to this story of which the essence is of her as a person. When she transitioned from being a patient to becoming a friend was probably a blurred line, but I would say it was when I introduced her as such at the wedding reception.

I admire her stamina and her resilience in the face of adversity, but most of all her indomitable will and her courage. Somewhere in my travels, I have lost the statue but that does not matter. I carry her memory with me and I know who the real Cinderella is. I am keenly aware that the best gift she gave me was not a statue, but "A piece of her heart." (Thank you too, Janis.)[10]

---

[10] Janis Joplin's 1968 hit, "Piece of My Heart."

# B.   One of My Heroes

Abe was a funny, thin and frail old man who used a wheelchair and in it he wandered all over the VA hospital. You could not miss him as he had a bald head and ears that stuck out like Dumbo's (an analogy he had heard before). After we had nodded in recognition or said hello a few times, he stopped me and asked what I did there. When I told him I was a psychologist, he asked what that was. In my explanation, I included that I "talked to people." His response was that he was people and why didn't I talk to him. Rather than explain that I needed a consult from his doctor and some diagnosis that would warrant my attention, I just said "sure" and suggested we have coffee together. I thought the meeting would be a "one-off" just to appease him.

Instead it began a wonderful friendship that often included coffee sessions together at least once a week. He always wanted to pay since he understood that usually I charged for my "talking." After some discussion, we finally agreed that friends should trade off who paid. When I got married, he received an engraved invitation to attend the wedding and reception. This delighted him and he accepted. Unfortunately the transportation he had arranged failed at the last moment. I did not find out about it until it was too late, something we both regretted. I missed him being there.

His story was quite a bit longer than any brief telling such as this could ever cover, but over the course of time I heard most of it. He had been a high-ranking enlisted man in the Navy and, as he told me, a huge strapping figure of a man. This was hard to see in his current one-hundred pound frame, but his medical history and stories supported it. I read much of his hospital chart, but never added a word to it.

He would not have said it himself, but I recognized that he had probably been a good father surrogate to many young seamen, albeit very tough. He said that many times rather than bring young sailors up on formal charges, he took them aside "to pound a little sense in them." Once after he won an offshore poker game, three men jumped him as he was returning to the ship. He said he gave them all a "what for" and then, "left them on the ground to contemplate the evil of their ways." For all this toughness, he still teared up when he talked about his wife, "now passed these many years before." He spoke of his regret that they never had children, and especially not having a son of his own. He was as open a person as I have known, and we shared on a level that is unusual for people of such different ages and backgrounds. In some respects, I suppose he was another of my surrogate fathers and I, another of the sons he never had.

This is a man I respected, admired, and was glad to call a friend. I wish I had been more comfortable to tell him this at the time. My next job was in another city so I lost contact with him. I suspect he roamed the hospital corridors and eventually found someone else for whom he made it their job to talk with him. Abe, I salute you.

# C.   Joe

Joe was once a policeman in Peoria, Illinois, and I met him there in the VA Clinic. His physician thought I might help Joe with some of the side effects of his medical condition. He was often nervous and no medication seemed to help for this condition. After I had been seeing him regularly for a while, I realized there was not much I could do for him as a psychologist. I did notice that he needed to get out of the house more often. One of his problems was that he had always been a very active man and when he sat at home too much, he became bored and "fidgety."

I discharged him from my care as a patient and began picking him up on Saturday mornings. This was a time when I would usually take my sons fishing or go on other weekend adventures. If the outings improved his medical problems, I didn't notice it, but by then we had become friends and he was good company. His wife Irene began inviting us in for coffee when we returned and she always had a homemade cake ready for the boys. The couple had never had children, but soon they became surrogate grandparents and "adopted" our sons. Joe was a musician and he taught the boys to play simple tunes on the organ. Eventually both Joe and Irene were included in many of our family outings. After a year of much resistance on our part, they finally insisted on occasionally sitting with our children when my wife and I went out for the evening. Both they and the boys benefitted from the increased contact.

I do not think I was ever in Joe's company when at least a few people who had known him from the past did not come up and greet him. It was clear that they liked and respected him. This gave me an opportunity to see Joe as the man they had once known. Many of them remembered him from his days on the local police force. A few of these old acquaintances were not embarrassed to say that they first met Joe when he arrested them. One man said that he was convinced not to mess with Joe after he saw him pick up a jackhammer with one hand. Another man talked about what a powerful man Joe was in character as well as physical strength, and how the word on the street was that he was fair, but it was best never to cross him. I believed this to be true considering the strength of his character.

After I received a promotion, I moved across the country and we lost touch with each other. We corresponded for a while, but their letters stopped coming and mine went unanswered. Eventually I was told by a mutual acquaintance that Joe and Irene had died. It was a privilege to have known them both.

# D. Two Beautiful Boys

The two boys in the title were hospitalized with serious congenital disorders that left their bodies twisted and often unwilling to respond even to their owners' most basic commands. If I had worked with the boys at the same time, I would have liked to introduce them to each other. I know they would have gotten along well. Perhaps because they had always lived with their physical limitations, they accepted them and made the best of what they had.

## Ronny

Red-haired and freckled, Ronny was an image of Tom Sawyer. He was about fourteen years old. One time when I was staying overnight at the children's hospital, we were talking. He asked if I was there to help patients with their problems. I replied, yes, I was there to help and I hoped I might do so for him. I asked if there was a problem he would like to discuss. He then asked for assurances that if he told me something, I would promise not to laugh when I heard it, and I would not tell anyone else. I promised. I hope he is alive today and if he reads this, I believe I do not now break my promise because I have sufficiently disguised his identity.

He said that sometimes he got excited, "You know; down there." I did know. He explained that when the lights went out and he tried to masturbate, all went well until he got close to the end. Then he could no longer control his hand and it would fly off. It left him frustrated and angry. We talked about this more and, I confess, I had no good answer for him. I would not insult him with empty platitudes. His life was difficult; in this area as in most others, he faced great challenges. I knew that one of the young student nurses often talked with him in his room so I asked about this. He seemed to breathe a sigh of relief that I had introduced this topic. It was something that really bothered him. She was not much older than he was and yet he knew that no matter how friendly she was to him, she would always be out of his reach, literally. He said that sometimes when she bent over to help him, he could see down her blouse and that did not help his situation much. I asked if it would perhaps be better if she were not as friendly. He thought about it for a moment and with a smile said that maybe it was better for her to come around, even if it did cause problems for him later.

I was able to help him with one concern by correcting one of the most stupid threats ever made to boys. Some groups teach that if people masturbate, they will go blind. "Would he?" I told him that this assertion was completely false and without any basis in fact. He seemed greatly relieved. I then leaned forward a little and in a whisper continued, "But of course it helps if you stop when you have to start wearing these." Then I slyly removed my glasses. After a second we both roared with laughter. At least I knew that in one area I had been able to help him.

I subsequently met his father who told me that Ronny had told him about our conversation, including the joke about the glasses, and he appreciated this. He said that he had not known how to approach the "whole situation" as he put it. He was glad that he and his son could now more comfortably discuss sex together. One suggestion he ran by me was the possibility of providing Ronny with a "sex worker." It did not take much thought to know that the facility would not sanction this. Perhaps in future he might have done so privately. What do you think of this solution?

# Frank

Frank was a slightly younger boy, but in many ways he was equally challenged physically. Unfortunately, Ronny had already returned home by the time Frank was admitted because I think the two of them would have made a wonderful team. I do not know how to communicate this well except to say that Frank radiated an absolute beauty. It shone from his inside out. You could not be with him and not feel good. Most of the staff quickly became aware of this and commented about it. As if to contradict his physical limitations, he was able to give something to everyone with whom he came in contact. Even as I write this bit of hyperbole, I am not sure of any other way to describe his effect on people. I do not know that I have ever been in the presence of a saint, but I do think that this must be what it would feel like.

It was my last night to stay over at the hospital; once again I was moving to a new position. I had talked with Frank before, but this being my last opportunity, I told him what a wonderful gift I thought he had. He thanked me and said this was not the first time he had heard something similar. I asked him if he had an explanation for the cause of his disposition and how people responded to him. He replied: "You should meet my Mom; she taught me." I tried to obtain an explanation, but he seemed lost for additional words. I did not feel comfortable to push with more questions. Now I wish that I had done so. I never did meet his mother, but I would have liked to know her. She must have been quite an unusual person. It may sound very strange to say this, but if Frank were a guru, I would have been his disciple. I still would.

# E.    I Remember Them

Of course there are more people who are among my favorites, but the following four are at the top of the list. I am keeping their stories to a minimum. Perhaps I selfishly do not want to share them with anyone. Maybe another time.

## Hope

I saw Hope in therapy for three years. She was diagnosed with a borderline personality disorder. This may be accurate, but it hardly begins to describe her as a person. More to the point would be to highlight her strength of character, constancy of painful effort to survive, and indomitable will.

During one particularly difficult period, I received frequent phone calls regarding Hope, informing me she was in trouble, again. She was often in the emergency clinic with superficial, but painful self-inflicted cuts. She had listed me as her emergency contact and she directed the staff to call Dr. Boeringa, i.e., me. I would explain to them that I was not a medical doctor but her psychologist. I took a risk and advised the physician in charge to clean the cuts, suture them if necessary, slap a bandage on them and send her home. I would then ask to talk with her. I reminded her to go to work at her department store job the next day, and to keep our next appointment. My support seemed very important to her and she always followed my advice. Once she sat outside my door all night so as not to disturb me, but to keep from doing anything to hurt herself. She didn't tell me until a week later. I was always afraid that one day I would make a wrong call. I also felt that my continued trust in her was an important factor in her healing. Thankfully, she survived the worst times and slowly began to grow stronger. By mutual consent, we stretched out our sessions from twice a week to once a week and then every two weeks. Eventually she improved enough that by mutual consent I discharged her from my care. She struggled with a terrible history, but she never gave up. I hope that now she is somewhere enjoying a wonderful retirement.

# Ben

Ben was a man who somehow reached thirty even after several serious suicide attempts and a record of being more in than out of mental hospitals. Overall, he was still one of the most positive and cheerful persons I have ever known. According to his description of them, half of his family was diagnosable as mentally ill and probably all of these with some form of a schizophrenic disorder. As he put it, the other half were just strange. He kept trying to work rather than be on welfare even though, as I repeatedly told him, employment would probably terminate his benefits and it would be very difficult to reinstate them. He loved to help others and he acted like he was the eternal Boy Scout. I read the records of some of his extremely violent and out-of-control episodes that led to hospitalization, but I never saw evidence of such behavior. If he ever felt he was losing control, he quickly had me or another practitioner admit him to the hospital. Usually, however, he was able to function outside on heavy doses of psychotropic medication. If he had not been a patient, I think I would have liked to have had him as a friend. I believe he was, as few are, a truly good person, all the more so for his liabilities.

# Sadie

The only complaints Sadie had were that she felt that nobody wanted her anymore and she felt useless. At the clinic where I worked, she badgered her physician for a referral to mental health. This doctor seemed only too glad to have Sadie transferred from her caseload to mine. After the first few sessions, she insisted on weekly appointments with me even though I repeatedly told her that she had no psychological reason to continue. For the next three months, I heard amazing stories of the rich and exciting life she had led and famous people she had known. Invented or not, I never found out. But at this stage of her life, she did have serious problems. Her career as an elementary school teacher was over. She was having difficulties "making ends meet" on her meager pension. At one time she earned a little extra money playing the organ for services at a local church, but then they replaced her and now she did not even have a place to practice in order to maintain her skills. There seemed little I could do to help, but then by chance I met someone who attended a church that needed an organist. They could pay but not much. It was not difficult to put the two together. Suddenly she had a purpose, a routine schedule and friends. She left me of her own accord as a patient but a few months later invited me to her first public recital, and of course I attended. She frequently stopped by to say hello after that. Sometimes in order to help, psychologists must step out of predefined roles.

# F.   Clyde

The last is often the best and this is, but in this case it is also the most difficult. It is the story of transformation from a patient to a friend that I came to know and love. Clyde had some chronic and severe medical problems that he lived with as best he could and he eventually died from them. I saw many medical patients and would talk with them or sometimes use relaxation training or biofeedback to help them deal with pain. I did so with Clyde. In the course of my work with him, I also came to hear about his life and I was impressed with his intellect and his insights. In return, I think I helped him make some adjustments in his life that helped him. Seeing me was just the excuse he needed and soon he was too busy with things he enjoyed doing and was too improved to continue our appointments.

Finally I told him that he had graduated and no longer needed me as a therapist. He was upset until I told him that we could instead be friends if he wanted this. He did, although it took him a while to adjust to the change in relationship. We did not see each other as often, but when we did, it was always a treat for me and I hope it was for him. Our two families met for ice cream once, he gave my sons some well-crafted wooden toy cars that he had made, and we shared a similar, if sometimes "evil" sense of humor. I eventually left Idaho to move to a new job in Houston and when he and his wife visited there, we met for lunch.

Then one day he called and told me he was very sick and knew he was dying. He asked if I would be his therapist again as I was the helper he knew best. Yes, of course I would do this but it would be a personal not a professional relationship. I would do it as his good friend. We talked on the phone as long as he wanted and was able. Once we agreed to each drink the same favorite wine together while we talked during our regular Saturday meeting, he in Idaho, and I in Texas. By then he was too sick to enjoy the wine. I know that I tried to keep it from him, but I cried at least once that day as I realized I would not see him again. Soon after that he died. In unimagined ways I keep his trust, and I continue to honor his friendship. The toys he gave my sons, I was later able to give to the children of his son. The circle remains unbroken.

# G.   A Closing Note on this Chapter

You will notice that I seem to keep picking up these used-to-be-patients-who-are-now-friends.   I   make   no apologies. I not only know all about dual relationships, I have given workshops on them. I am very aware of the need to never exploit people no matter what their relationship is to me, professional or otherwise, and I do not think I have done so to the people I have written about in these stories. I believe any of my actions would sustain inquiry from an ethical review board. I also know that for me, people do not have "Patient" stamped across their foreheads in permanent ink. They are people first. Where a line is drawn, when and where it is ever crossed, or to what degree, is an individual decision based upon the situation at the time. In other cases and with different circumstances, I have maintained the boundaries with unyielding firmness.

# XII.    THE ONE ABOUT ME

Now it is my turn. It is my prejudice that in order to become a good psychotherapist you have to experience the other side of the equation: to be a patient in therapy yourself. Accordingly, and because at times I have also hit bumps in the road of life, I have been in therapy. Additionally I maintained an ongoing relationship with a mentoring colleague I could go to when I felt I was lost or in over my head with a particular case.

Does therapy work? It is very difficult to establish both reliable and valid outcome measures for psychotherapy because it is hard to obtain objective measures. Therapists may be in the best position to observe subtle changes in attitude, mood and behavior, but they are obviously biased. The success levels reported by patients are often based on either subjective satisfaction or cognitive dissonance. If you are unfamiliar with the latter term, in this usage it means that if you put a lot of time, effort and money, especially money, into something, it MUST be worth it. If not, then what does this say about your investment? Longitudinal studies are expensive and it is impossible to know if subsequent changes in a person's life resulted from the therapy or if they would have occurred even without it. A person may spend an hour a week with you; the rest of the time they are subject to multiple other influences. Ultimately, the question "Does therapy work?" may be answered by whether the recipient deems the therapy worthwhile and by the criteria they have established to judge its success.

217

I can say that in my case, therapy was worth it and I received my time and money's worth. Did it transform me and am I an entirely different person today because of it? No, but if you pay to go to a movie or concert, even though you have an emotionally moving experience, you still do not expect the buzz to last forever. Major surgery can be a painful and expensive experience, but sometimes it does not solve the problem. If it relieves the problem only a little, or only for a while, does that mean it should not have been attempted? When it fails, you still must pay. There is even a risk that you will end up worse than when you started. Finally, sometimes people get better even without any interventions. This is true of any disorder, medical or psychological.

Therapy benefitted me and perhaps by extension, it benefitted my patients. It helped me grow in many ways. When you read the following, see what you think.

# A. Alexander

In teaching and when I supervise students, I try to insist that beginning therapists should have their own therapy. I had mine. I tried to kid myself that it was only another part of my training, but it is hard to fool yourself: I needed it. I think I am both a better person and a better therapist because of it. Still, there are no miracles here; there are many people who will tell you I should go back to training wheels. And these are the people who love me. I continue to be a jerk at times.

I will recount a very few experiences with my first therapist in order to illustrate some of the feelings I had in therapy and some of the things I learned about myself. I do not intend to share everything with you. Or anyone, ever. I will call my therapist Ed because he Ed-ucated me. See? I have yet to be cured of the temptation of punning.

My own therapy allowed me to see the process from the other side of the veil. Two situations were especially useful to me in my development as a therapist. In the first one my session with Ed was scheduled just after lunch and I arrived right on time. Through his open office door I noticed that he was reading a newspaper and when I knocked he looked, at least to me, annoyed at having to put it down. I sat through half the session fuming: How dare he? Was I less important than his crummy paper? However, I could not initially bring myself to complain. I depended upon this man for help and what is more I wanted him to like me and to be impressed with me. Confronting him felt like a huge risk. It was a quandary. As pissed off as I was, I still did not want to alienate him. I finally gathered my courage and told him what I was feeling. He did not make a pro forma apology and move on as most people might have. He said he was guilty as

219

charged and hit me with the standard therapist line: How did that make me feel? In the weeks ahead we spent hours on how I felt, both in being dependent on powerful authority figures in my life and in resenting their power over me. I still have issues with this, but I have fewer tendencies to act out in destructive ways.

Some of the more astute among you will at this point have an "Aha!" moment and try to drag in what you have noticed as my frequent tendencies to collect father surrogates. Guilty as charged. Read on.

In many instances in therapy, both my own and in my work with patients, I learned the power of pulling one small string. The trick was to identify what was most important and to then focus on it and to interpret any resistance this elicited. As in my example given above, what I did not want to do most was what I needed to do most. In this and in other ways, I began to get an inkling of how my patients might feel and how they might experience therapy. I was given a firsthand lesson.

This seemingly small event taught me about transference, fear of rejection, wanting to be liked no matter what it cost, and that my worst anxieties would seldom come to pass. I learned about confrontation and about communication. That was probably the single most important piece of my therapy. Even though I tired of talking about the newspaper incident and I resisted each new facet of my personality it brought out, Ed continued to pursue it. I hope my own patients received as good a result when I pushed them to where they needed to go, even though they hated it every step of the way. Even if at the time they considered me a royal pain. Think about the story: Taking out the Garbage.

The next incident is amusing as I recall it, but at the time it seemed to be a Big Deal to me. Austin in the mid-1960s was like a small town, especially on campus. There were groups of people with similar interests and many of them were interrelated. Because of this, it was no surprise for me to go to a party one night and find Ed there. I was not sure if I could be comfortable around my therapist and I worried what he might see in my behaviors, but he seemed relaxed about my presence so I decided to stay. As the evening wore on I noticed that Ed was obviously getting a little drunk. He was having a very good time, but he also seemed especially and unnecessarily loud to me. I was incensed. How could he, a therapist, and what is more MY therapist, deport himself like this! I depended on him and at the time I thought I needed him for my strength. I expected him to remain the perfect person I had imagined him to be. I was appalled to find that he was human too and might have a few chinks in his armor. I left the party early.

In the next therapy session I expressed my feelings about seeing him, as it were, dressed in the emperor's new clothes. I told him I had put him on a pedestal but he had disappointed me. Then and in subsequent therapy sessions he patiently helped me see that maybe I did so because of my perceived need for him to be perfect. Even more slowly, it became apparent that this tendency was a pattern in my life, beginning with my father (surprise, surprise!). I was able to accept that it was not the responsibility of either of us to meet my unrealistic expectations. My task was to set realistic expectations for my own life and then to have the courage to try to meet them, and to accept the responsibilities for their success or failure.

Patients have many projections and transferences they try to place on their therapists; we could never meet them all. It is better to be able to forgive our own shortcomings and cut some slack for our failures than to set so high a standard that we can never meet it. Who placed that bar so high we could never reach it anyway?

Another example: How far do I feel I must I go to maintain the illusion for my own patients? If a patient sees me in public when I am wearing my "grubbies," will they still respect me? Should I care? When I ask such questions, hopefully I remember that it is my own self-importance that is at stake here, or my silly need to be put on my own pedestal; I have created my own fantasies.

Soon after he received his Doctorate, my friend Kevin had concerns about being seen in a store wearing the dirty work clothing in which he had just mowed his yard. We both laughed about this, but it struck a responsive chord in me. Fortunately, some of us have outgrown the need to maintain outward appearances. In addition, society has changed toward much more casual attitudes--some might say too casual--about one's style of dress, or undress as the case maybe.

So? Enough stories for now. Have I been cured? Well no, but therapy helped and I still advocate it for beginning therapists as well as for we more mature types who hit a snag in our lives. Certainly there are those who believe they have found The Answer for their lives, whatever *that* may be. More power to them. I remain content with my growing collection of "little" answers. So far they seem to be working and growing. I hope you have not been disappointed in my stories and especially the one about me.

# B.  A Premature Postscript

This about wraps it up for now. You have read something about how I am with patients, as well as how I am as a patient. Through using your own insight, you already know a lot about me. We therapists talk about being a Tabula Rasa or Blank Slate, and we try to keep ourselves hidden from our patients: the better to encourage projection and transferences I suppose. Besides, it is not supposed to be about us, now is it?

You always find us out anyway.

Near the end of therapy with a person, I used to share a little more of myself with them. I would let the veil slip a bit. My theory was that I was helping them to demythologize me and balance any perceived distances between us as real people. I then realized that I was the one who needed the dose of reality, not them. They had already seen beneath the mask. I hope this book completes the process.

All I can say is that I have tried to be honest with both of us.


Namaste

# C.  Other Duties as Assigned

This section is not about specific patients, but rather it provides some indication of the wide range of clinical and professional activities that have always made my work so varied, interesting and fulfilling.

My career offered me intimate contact with people from so many ages, cultures, histories and walks of life that it would be rare for me to meet most of them under any other circumstances. In their own unique way, each of them has enriched my life. For one thing, knowing them helped me overcome some of the stereotypes and prejudices that might otherwise have persisted in me had I not met these people. I had a peek behind the curtain of their history, and began to understand the elements that shaped their lives, just as surely as the different experiences had molded my own. My various employments have opened a number of avenues for me to explore, a variety of roles to play, a broad range of formally assigned duties, and the independent activities I have invented for myself. They have also provided extensive travel and the opportunity to live in a variety of places.

My employment allowed me to take on unassigned tasks that interested me. If I saw a need for something, I would try to fulfill it. I have always followed the rule that it is better to ask forgiveness than permission. When in doubt, I just did it. My greatest luck has been that I never had a job I did not enjoy; there was always something new and interesting to explore, learn, or turn into an opportunity. That list included everything from being a "white collar" professional to the times when I literally dug ditches. Once in the middle of winter in New Mexico, I was in the bottom of an eight-foot mud hole with snow and dirt falling on my head and I knew that if I had to do this work for the rest of my life, I could find satisfaction in it. Compared to that experience, my life as a clinical psychologist was a cinch. Either way, I am grateful for my good fortune.

# 1. Employee Assistance

I found Employee Assistance Programs (EAP) to be especially rewarding. Most of the people I saw had only minor problems and it was good to be able to help my fellow employees. In this position it is especially important to maintain confidences. This is particularly the case when working with employees where so many people interact closely with each other and gossip is often rampant. Once in a particularly sensitive situation, I was even allowed to see participants off station in my private practice office to keep a problem from becoming public knowledge. An amusing example of how well I was able to maintain client privacy is typified in the following example. Three women were having lunch together when one of them said that she had to leave early. The other two naturally asked where she was going. They already knew that she was having "issues" with her boyfriend so she sheepishly told them that she was seeing me about this problem. Another of the women told her not to be embarrassed and admitted that I was counseling her as well. At this, the third woman blurted out that they might as well make it unanimous; I was helping her quit smoking. Then they all had a good laugh together. Each of them independently told me the story and thanked me for keeping confidences so well.

A related EAP assignment was to assist in the development of a dress code. I worked closely with several people including union officials and management. It turned out well. When finished, we introduced the new rules in a hospital-wide, hilarious fashion show. Any remaining tapes of my own performance I will gladly pay to have destroyed. The first problem arose when a week later one rather buxom woman showed up wearing a see-through blouse.

This was a clear (no pun intended) violation of the rules; someone had to discuss this with her and persuade her to either change her style of dress or be sent home from work. I asked, "Why me?" Her male supervisor said he would rather eat glass than talk with her about it, and my boss told me I needed to do it. Specifically, I was assigned "because I was a psychologist," and "I knew how to do these things." No, I did not. I met with the lady, and yes, she was wearing The Blouse. Not since I asked for my first date have I stammered through anything as difficult. She did not make it any easier as she persisted in not understanding the problem. I think she knew and enjoyed my discomfort. In the end I told her that what she was wearing was very attractive, but that she was distracting too many of the male employees. I suggested that management would appreciate it if she would wear something a little more modest and less attention drawing. She agreed, I think especially since her boyfriend had already objected to it and she "thought" he might be jealous.

Compared to that, the next one was easy. An older Southern Gentleman persisted in touching everyone as he talked with them, male or female. It was a cultural habit of his and unintentional, but it remained a clear violation of sexual harassment guidelines. I explained the problem and he said yes, he understood, but did I understand? He maintained it was just the way he had grown up. As he said this he reached over to pat my knee and assured me he that he wouldn't do it anymore. He evidently still had a way to go.

Once I served as co-chair of the Union-Management Partnership Committee. I thought that this assignment would provide an opportunity to do some good in the hospital and, by collaborating with the union, we could develop some win-win programs and share our common

227

objectives. In retrospect, that was naïve, but we did manage to get along in several areas. Most of the people I worked with on both sides of the fence genuinely wanted to do what was right for the employees and the patients we served. Clearly I was not functioning here as a psychologist, but I found that many of the principles applicable to good management depended a lot on the same ones discovered by or used in psychology.

## 2.  Mediation

The first time I heard about mediation was from a friend who was a pioneer in the field. She told me the story of one of her cases. A couple was engaged in a bitter child custody battle and appeared before a judge who asked the couple to come up to the bench. She then asked each one of them if they loved their children. They tripped over each other in protesting how much they loved and would do anything for them. When they had finished, she leaned forward and said to them in measured tones, "Well, let me tell you something. I DO NOT love your children." When the couple recovered from this shock, she explained that she believed that they, who loved their children so much, should logically be the ones to decide what was really best for them. It should not be a stranger who did not even know the children. With this in mind, she instructed them to decide the children's welfare and future with the help of a mediator. Gavel down.

When the hospital offered to have me trained in mediation at a local law school, I jumped at the opportunity. At the conclusion of the course, I was even given release time from my VA duties to provide mediation at a county court for a few hours each week. The hospital administration also frequently called upon me to mediate cases that might otherwise result in adverse actions by management or in a grievance from the union.

I enjoy doing therapy, but I must admit that in many cases I would rather do mediation. It is often much more satisfying as the result can often be observed right on the spot. In fact, in the cases I participated in, when an agreement was reached between the two parties, the judge who assigned the case would immediately "make it so."

Sometimes you win; sometimes you lose. One amusing case that did not end well involved a man who demanded that the minister of his church be fired because he did not preach according to the man's particular, unorthodox beliefs. I do not know how this dispute even came to court, but it did. The judge assigned it to me with a shake of his head. The minister was quite conciliatory, but the man remained adamant, and he also refused to follow the rules of mediation. He just sought a platform from which to complain. I declared it a hopelessly locked situation. The judge was not happy to see the two parties return and he swiftly denied the man's case. Thankfully, most mediation I was involved with ended much better.

## 3.    Grief Counseling

In any large organization, there are inevitably deaths among employees and I was frequently asked to do grief counseling on an individual or a workgroup basis. The co-workers of the deceased were almost as traumatized as the family, so I would provide an intervention as soon as possible at the worksite. Causes of death included heart attacks, motor vehicle accidents, murders, self-inflicted deaths, and one instance of murder-suicide.

The first time I was asked to counsel a workgroup, I called a previous supervisor of mine for advice. He told me to stick with the five R's: Resistance; Repression; Remembrances; Regrets; and Resentments. Over the years this formula proved to be useful and the progression was often predictable.

There might be some initial Resistance in the need for a session at all, or in the necessity of bringing in a complete outsider. Some people chose to opt out or were told that if they came, they did not have to speak. Repression is technically more akin to Denial, but since Denial does not fit the neat progression of R's and Repression does, I continue to use the latter. It is the "I can't believe it, I just spoke to him last week" expression reflecting the difficulty of accepting that this really happened. Next, there was always an outpouring of fond Remembrances and anecdotes about the person: Variations on the theme of, "They had been everyone's friend and a veritable saint." This slides into the Regrets of "I wish I had," and, "We were always going to but now we never can." Alternatively, in some cases there is the hindsight Regret of should-have-seen-it-comings.

231

At first I was unsure why Resentment was included, but after hearing it surface several times, I do think it is a common feeling even though sometimes people have difficulty expressing it. It may be heard in comments such as "if only they had..." or "you know I hate to say it but, they always did" drive too fast, get too angry, neglect their health, etc. I have also seen real anger expressed by survivors for being left behind. They were now alone and forced to deal with all of the implications of their loved one's death. At first Resentment came as a shock. Now I listen for it.

The nicest session I have attended was one in which a colleague and I co-led a group and in closing he asked participants to form a circle, think of the departed friend for a moment and then celebrate his life and theirs with raised hands and a loud heartfelt "Yeah!" This request was a surprise for me as well as for the group, but I think it was healing for all of us.

## 4.    ER Duty

As Medical School Faculty in the Department of Psychiatry and Behavioral Sciences it was periodically my job to provide night duty supervision and instruction for medical students on the mental health rotation. They were assigned to the emergency room psychiatric evaluations and admissions area. We had an area of our own in which to see patients separated from the rest of the ER. It was a duty that could provide hours of boredom punctuated by moments of sheer panic. I liked using the time to spread the gospel of psychology among the students. I was often fortunate enough to work with Dr. Graham Reed and we began a friendship that lasted for many years. In quiet periods, we would make bets on who was more accurate in diagnosing patients as they approached down a long hallway. Then we would explain to the students why we made our judgments based on initial observations alone. We were frequently correct in our assessments. Often it was just showing off.

One night a bedraggled young woman came in with ambiguous complaints and we were concerned that she could be suicidal. We asked her to wait to see if the symptoms became clearer. Meanwhile she emptied our pockets with requests for money for the snack machines. Eventually we decided that she was safe to leave and we scheduled a follow-up appointment for the next day. At 2 a.m., we had seen our last patient and I was finally free to go home. As I drove past the Galveston seawall, I saw emergency vehicles with flashing lights parked near a pier. My first panicked thought was that we had guessed wrong and that our patient had killed herself soon after leaving us. I talked to the crew and learned that they were indeed retrieving a body, but one that had fallen off an oil derrick several days previously. A relief, and a reminder that sometimes the decisions we made could be life or death.

The mental health deputies in Galveston are also law officers and they are very well trained in each of these areas. Ortega was a very large muscular man who had hands about the size of a catcher's mitt. I once saw a plus-sized woman haul off and give him a slap that would have floored me. He brushed it off as he might have a mosquito and only gently commented, "Now Betsy, let's calm down please." Once a man pulled a knife on me and I was trying to talk him into putting it down. My gentle giant stood back just far enough to let me be in charge, but if needed he was plainly close enough to intervene. I appreciated his support and respect. It was good to have Ortega around, especially when patients were considering violence. The man finally gave me the knife and orderlies took him to the psychiatry ward. Coffee was on me.

One man who was extremely high on PCP, or "Angel Dust," as it was known on the street, was brought in by four police officers. All of the officers had their uniforms somewhat torn and a few of them were showing the beginnings of bruises. The man was now lying on a gurney in four-point leather restraints. The officers told me that it had taken three tasers, or stun guns, to take him down. Usually when they brought in a person who was angry or agitated, I would ask the patient if they thought they could control themselves and speak to me more calmly. If they said "yes," I had the handcuffs or other restraints removed. They usually agreed and I earned the beginnings of trust and the goodwill of having done them a small favor. Knowing this, with a wide grin on his face, one police officer asked, "How about it, Doc; you want us to cut this guy loose like usual so you can talk to him?" This time I decided I would wait until after he was detoxed to interview him. Or better yet, the task might be delayed until someone else's shift.

A very large and very manic woman, high on life, a bit of booze and who knows what else on board to help it along, arrived on her own steam one quiet night. She instantly proceeded to "do the dozens" on the entire ER staff. She was extremely clever, accurate, and outrageously funny; that is, until she came to outline one's own characteristics and peculiarities. The staff let her continue for a while until the head of the ER came out of the office to see what the cause of the uproar was. He quickly put an end to the show but not before, to the amusement of all, the patient verbally skewered him to the bone. There were quiet nights when I often wished she would pay us another visit, but she never returned. And no, strangely enough, I do not recall the particular ditty she spun for me, but I recall that it made me both laugh and wince.

Another very disturbed patient declined my offer for her to spend the night in our comfortable mental ward and she immediately took off, running through dimly lit and deserted corridors. The police and whatever staff we could spare set out to bring her back. Guided by her manic screams, we finally found her. Following very clear legal guidelines, she easily met the criteria for an involuntary commitment. With a physician's signature and mine, the necessary papers were prepared. As I tried to do with all patients I admitted, I visited her in the hospital the next morning. She was back on a medication and much calmer. She only half remembered me, but she did thank me for coming to see her. She also suggested we enter into a sexual act that to this day I am not sure is possible. I left her with my best wishes.

## 5.    False Positives/Negatives

A false positive is when a decision is made that something is true and it turns out not to be. An example is a drug test report stating you took a drug when you did not; or a positive pregnancy test is wrong so it is time to try again. A false negative is when you took the drug, but the test fails to detect it and you skate...this time. Or the pregnancy test said no way, and here you are with a growing belly. It follows that there are also true positives and true negatives as well. The drug or pregnancy test is then accurate in both cases, or in other words the decision is spot on for either one.

The reason I bring these up is because of a childcare worker who molested several children. The newspaper printed each new development on the front page and repeatedly asked how this could happen. The public was outraged and, since people always look to blame someone else, the onus fell on the facility management as to why they didn't screen applicants better. The attorneys representing opposing sides in the hearing wanted to know if psychological testing could identify child molesters. Several experts--attorneys and mental health workers--including myself, were requested to provide a seminar on the problem.

Forgetting for a moment the complexities of reliability, validity, sensitivity and specificity, most tests, including medical ones, have some margin of error; the question is how great and what the consequences are. Measuring any abstract quality, such as a potential to commit an act, increases by a large factor the difficulties of predicting its future occurrence, and the possibility of wrong categorizations.

A test with ninety-percent accuracy in sorting potential molesters from non-molesters would be a miracle in the first place. You would hardly expect pedophiles to truthfully answer the question: "I enjoy touching little children; True or False." But say you tested one-hundred applicants and there were ten molesters among them. Of the ninety acceptable workers, there would be eighty-one who had a clean bill of health; enough to pick from. However, the test would weed out only nine of the ten pedophiles. One would escape the net and if hired be especially dangerous because they would be above suspicion in the future since they had passed the test. And what happens to the nine people who are one-hundred percent innocent but "flunked?" Given the ease of obtaining information in our present society, how long would it be before they were labeled as molesters and suffered the consequences?

My own opinion on how to predict what will happen next is to bet on what happened before. In my experience, past behaviors best predict future actions.

# 6. Testifying

There was a time when I could have made a living by administering psychological assessments to defendants on trial, parents who wanted custody, the children they wanted custody of, and kids who missed the Gifted and Talented Program by one or two points. I would soon have a well-earned reputation as a Hired Gun. No thanks.

I do not like to testify in court. It is my nature to try to see all sides of every situation and be "fair" and, in my opinion, that is seldom what attorneys or their clients are looking for. When asked to testify as an expert witness, I would double or triple my usual fees, and demand portal-to-portal and wait-time payment. Even that didn't work sometime. An attorney acquaintance once told me that compared to his fees I came cheap. I would never volunteer to be an expert witness or to testify in any case, but if subpoenaed, you have to go anyway. One example will give the flavor of why I hated to testify.

I had begun seeing pain patients and my experience with one man who was injured at work gave me new insight into the game. His attorney sent him to me as part of the documentation of his pain and suffering. Even though he felt capable of some activity he was told by his attorney to never be seen mowing the lawn or doing anything else that would weaken his claims. He told me that company spies had tried to photograph him at these "forbidden" activities. As a result, he was afraid to leave the house. The employer's insurance company sent him to appointments in distant cities hoping he would not show; when he did show, he was informed that his appointment had been cancelled.

Nevertheless, at least one physician who did not even meet with him wrote a report documenting that he was able to return to work.

Eventually his case came to trial and I was subpoenaed to testify as an Expert Witness. After being sworn in, I had to be formally qualified—stipulated, I think the term is--as to my education, training, and credentials, and accepted by both parties.

In any interchanges with me, my patient's attorney always referred to me respectfully as "Doctor Boeringa." When the company lawyer started questioning me, he began by "clarifying my status" and said, "I notice you have been referred to as Doctor, but you are not a medical doctor are you?" I answered no, and he proceeded: "Well then, *Mister* Boeringa." From then on it got worse. There was the usual trick question of asking how much I was being paid for my opinions in favor of the man. Answer: I was being paid but only for my time and expert testimony to the court. He did not call me a liar, but he often managed to come quite close. At no time did the injured man's attorney jump up with vehement objections Perry Mason style. I was on my own, and in a very angry mood.

As I was leaving the building, the insurance company attorney called to me: "Doctor Boeringa, could I have a word with you?" I was determined to slug him if he said one thing out of line, but all he said was, "You did a great job in there. I wonder if I may have your card and call you to testify some time. I do a lot of cases like this." How many ways can you say no?

# 7. Workshops and Mandated Training Seminars

I cannot count the number of workshops and seminars I have presented; probably too many. My objection to most of them is that they are usually ineffectual and a large waste of everyone's time at best, if not altogether useless. But it was a part of my job and so I did them; oh yes, and I frequently got paid. The best part was when I was not only paid to do them, but I was able to travel to some nice locations.

My doctoral dissertation was on the relationship between stress and illness so I was often asked to give stress reduction workshops. As I suggested above, such events seldom change anyone's behavior. At best, they may reduce stress for a day by getting the attendees away from their normal routine. Period. Any benefits accruing from them last about as long as an aspirin. My opinion of course. I finally decided that since almost anything I did would accomplish this goal I would enjoy myself. From then on I tried to have the audience be as active as possible rather than just listening to me drone on. One favorite exercise was to find a large enough venue to trace a giant labyrinth on the floor and have them all walk it. This is a devise with a long and honored history beginning hundreds of years ago in Europe, and besides I was the expert; if I said it helped, then it helped.

Now a few words about Safety, Diversity, Sexual Harassment, Anti-Terrorism; Ethics; Violence in the Workplace, Recognizing Substance Abuse, and you add your own least favorite training topics. Many of you have probably sat through at least one session on these topics. You decide if they were effective. I do not think that people's basic attitudes or behaviors are very often changed by being forced to attend most of these sessions. What they primarily accomplish is to Cover the Butts of Management (CYA anyone?). They satisfy some federal or other regulatory requirement that training be given and documented. Yes, they are important topics, but they are not useful if all they are designed to do is counter potential claims that future offenders did not know the rules when they violated them. And yes, I "taught" these anyway, and when I had to attend them as a participant, I brought some office work or a book with me.

I honestly did try to make my workshops interesting and relevant, but often there was an established, rigid routine and I was not expected, sometimes not even allowed, to vary from it much. I know that my opinions as stated above are a bit inflammatory and the point is open to argument. I welcome any scientifically obtained, objective statistics to the contrary, especially when the information is part of a double-blind study. I hope this does not mean that now I will be asked to return the money I was paid to conduct these seminars.

I once learned a valuable lesson about how to conduct training when was I was paired with an out-of-town person I did not know. We were to present a two-day seminar on a fairly technical subject. I was grossly over-prepared and I thought I did a brilliant job of competently hitting every detail in my portion of the training. On the other hand, the other presenter regaled them with stories, wandered all over the landscape and, I think, threw in bits from a recycled lecture on an irrelevant subject. Much of the time, he had the audience laughing and he gave them long breaks. When the participant evaluations were tabulated, guess who they loved, and guess who they unanimously recommended to be asked to return next year? Did they learn anything from either of us? Who knows, but they sure liked him the most.

# XIII. CONCLUSION

For me, love has been a major theme of this book. It is about the many people for whom I once felt love, and as I write about them, I find that I still do. In English we use one word, "Love," to describe a rich and varied response to just about everything and every situation or relationship. We "love" people, pizza, exercise, inanimate machines, vague feelings, activities, and things so abstract I cannot even describe them here. It is in this sense that I loved many of my patients. I have sometimes been closer to them than to many of my dearest friends, and I often shared in their lives on a deeper level than most people are able to experience or would tolerate. After many years have gone by, I still care for these people, wonder about them, and have warm feelings when I remember them. It sounds like love to me. As I could not tell them then, I do so now with gratitude.

I think that in spite of any therapeutic skills I acquired in my professional education, at heart it is the quality of love, however defined, that often facilitates whatever cure that may have been effected. Maybe when reflected in a therapist's "love," people just begin to love themselves. Likewise, if the therapist demonstrates respect for the patient, the patient's self-respect may grow. I know this is a very unscientific, sloppily sentimental and embarrassingly mystic explanation so you can discard it out of hand if you like. I am not sure I always believe it either, but it seems to me as good an explanation as any. As you read or re-read the stories of these people, the problems

243

they bring, and their responses to our interactions, do consider the possibility that love plays a role in the outcome.

# XIV. APPENDIX

The remainder of the book addresses my approach to psychotherapy, and includes a collection of sayings I have found helpful. Over the years I have shared these with students to illustrate a point. I hope the information is helpful to you.

## A. Nuts and Bolts

# An Oversimplified Introduction to

# Psychotherapy—

# As Practiced By Me

# 1.    How Psychotherapy Works: I Don't Know

A piece of wisdom I heard once goes like this:

There are only two rules for success.

1. The first is to never tell everything you know.

2.

Cute isn't it? I would of course be glad to tell you what number two is, but as the chapter heading says: I really do not know. What is more, I maintain that no one knows; my suggestion is that you avoid anyone who says they do. Before you grow too judgmental of me as a psychologist, consider that we say physicians "practice" medicine. If one drug does not work, they try another; a drug that works for one patient may not work for another and vice versa. Some operations provide relief from the illness, some do not. Some drugs and interventions are essentially placebos; that is, they work no better than sugar pills. Some people get better just from interaction with a caring person to whom they attribute special skills or knowledge. This is what Freud would have called a Transference Cure. If it works, don't knock it. I can guarantee you that if you go to forty different psychotherapists, you will have forty different experiences. The miracle is that they might all work! Depending on the patient, I use several different theoretical and practical approaches. Often the methods are helpful but not always. Technically my style is known as Eclectic, more familiarly known as the "different strokes approach."

What I can tell you is that I have been in therapy. It worked for me and I have seen it work for other people. If I did not believe that it worked for many of my patients, I would have quit trying to help them and gone back to ditch digging.

# How Psychotherapy Works: What I DO Know

It is taught that the common response to a threat is either Fight or Flight. An often given example is that when faced with a saber- toothed tiger, our ancestors had to make one of those choices. I prefer to think of us as having four choices. I call it staying SAFE. That adds two more options. There is Submission; Avoidance; Fighting; or Escape. Today many of life's circumstances confront us with these same choices. In the face of a difficult situation do we give up, go around, get into a conflict or run away? A benign example could be when we see the office bore approach and opt for one of these actions: Submit to a long pointless story, Avoid by turning in the other direction, Fight by confronting them with your angry feelings or Escape to a meeting you suddenly remember. You can add your own examples, but the four SAFE reactions usually describe your options fairly well. Problems that bring people to therapy generally have these same characteristics. They feel trapped and rightly or wrongly believe that they have no options, or they cannot see them.

When you read about the people in this book, maybe you can see how they had gotten stuck, how that contributed to their problems, and how by changing their responses they could or did change their life. My assumption is that everyone who is unhappy would like to change. Often, they just do not know how to begin the process. I also believe that by the simple act of turning to someone else for help, they are to some extent, ready to make a change.

## 2.    A Few Things I Have Learned the Hard Way

In today's world it seems that everyone is boasting about being "Number One." T-shirts stupidly proclaim that Number Two is just the first place for losers. Multiple sources repeat that whatever it is in life that you might want, you deserve it. You can always have it your way. That may work with hamburgers; it does not often work as well in relationships. I am a bit old-fashioned. I do not believe that all must win and all must have prizes. I know that I am not Number One. That is not humility; it is reality. I used to tell my students that I was in the top 99% of my graduating class. Some of them instantly "got it," for some others it took a while. I have learned to accept who and what I am.

Often in the middle of a session with a patient, I have fervently wished that there was *someone* in the room who knew what they were doing. Then I would think of my graduate school supervisor who most shaped and guided my practice of therapy, and I would ask myself, "What Would Doctor Langston Do?"[11] But of course he was not there in the room to help me. I would imagine myself in supervision with him and ask the question WWDLD? The answer always came to me. Just as with my patients' experience, quite often I had known the answer all the time. I just needed someone to drag it out of me. Maybe today somewhere one of my ex-

---

[11] I was greatly saddened by the news of Doctor Langston's death. I have always looked up to and honored him, both as a teacher and as a friend.

patients may be asking themselves, "What Would Doctor Boeringa Do?" I hope they get the answer they need!

Early in my career I learned that patients seldom tell the whole truth, especially not in the beginning of our work together. The very things they fail to mention may be critical to their chance of success in therapy. Like a detective, I just assume they are keeping things from me. Then I go to work figuring out why it is so difficult for them to face the truth. Physicians tell me that their patients also withhold crucial health information, even when the facts might help the physician treat them more effectively or save their life.

We learn early in life to keep our secrets and the habit continues. Michael, did you break this window? No, Dad. Matthew, did you practice the trombone? Yes, Dad. Were you speeding? No, officer.

We are never sure when the truth may hurt us and so we conclude it may be better to err on the safe side and lie until we find out what the consequences might be. Likewise, many patients do not reveal why they have come for therapy until I can be tested and awarded a level of trust.

I learned that when in doubt, just shut up. This lesson was brought home to me strikingly whenever I had a bad cold or a sore throat and it hurt to talk. I did less talking. The less I spoke, the more the patients talked and the better they became. That was tough on my ego. At first I thought it was my job to open people up. Then I realized how dreadfully painful it can be once people do open up. It is my responsibility to help put them back together. Sometimes that is not easy. I think the analogy of a surgeon fits nicely here. Cutting a patient open can be rapid and fairly easy; fixing what is inside and sewing the patient back up again may require a lot more patience and skill.

My other awakening was that I needed to be healthy myself if I was to help others grow and change. A more difficult lesson was to discover that no matter what my patient had done, or how abhorrent I found it to be, I had to find some common ground with them. I could understand even the worst tendencies in others if I acknowledged some degree of those traits in me. In certain circumstances I might feel that I *could* do this thing, or experience the urge to do so.

I also needed to find something in each person I could like. I had to make a connection on a basic human level that allowed honest communication with them and I had to be concerned about their welfare. Why else would I want them to get better? How else could I work to accomplish this? Most importantly, I had to believe that at some level they too wanted to change.

Once I begin therapy with a person and a commitment on their part is made to change, and on my part to help them, I consider them to be my patient. For life. If they show up years later, I have an obligation to help them. Period. It also seems obvious that it is wrong to exploit a patient's trust in any way, or to promise them anything you might not be able to deliver.

## 3. Confidentiality: Ask but Don't Tell

I live with more secrets than most people. Over many years I have become a repository of so many people's secrets that they all swim together in my head, but I always keep them. So how is it that I now write about real people and real events? I have altered as many facts as I can that could lead to recognition. It is my intention that no patient ever be able to recognize themself in these pages with any certainty, or for anyone else to think that they recognize someone they know. Remember that many problems are similar.

In a very few instances, I have included a personal note to someone who thinks they might be the person described. Again, I intend that the details are changed enough and are sufficiently vague that no one can be certain it is them, or for anyone who knows them to guess. To all my patients: I hope that all of you are doing well and are happy. I wish I knew.

There is an interesting contradiction in doing psychotherapy. Even though I must maintain strict confidentiality, the patients do not have to do so. Even if they were with friends in a public place, some people always seemed to take pride in coming up to me and saying hello to "their shrink." I always kept these encounters short but not rejecting. I would never recognize them first lest it prove to be embarrassing. Of course I was polite if they began the conversation, and I would introduce them to my family if they were with me.

Once a woman came up to my wife at a party and introduced herself as one of my patients. She went on to describe in glowing terms how wonderful I was, a good listener and such a patient and caring person. She finally concluded by saying that it must be great to be married to me. My wife pointedly told the woman that she must have me mixed up with someone else; she did not recognize the person described.

The first time my young sons had an inkling of my job was when a man came up to us in a mall and called me Doctor Boeringa. My sons were quite surprised as they had not heard me addressed this way before. They asked, "Was I really a doctor?" I tried to explain that I was a PhD and that people in many fields might carry that title. Then, as I wanted to make sure that they understood, I asked them if they knew what that meant. One of them responded that sure he knew: I was a doctor too, but not the kind that helped anybody!

# 4.　Same and Different

The public is often unaware of the difference between a psychologist and a psychiatrist. My PhD, or Doctorate, is in clinical psychology, while a psychiatrist is first of all a medical doctor (MD). Psychiatrists have special advanced training in the medical treatment of mental disorders. I am not a medical doctor and therefore I cannot prescribe medications. If I think that a patient's condition warrants it, I refer them to a psychiatrist for an evaluation. Other competent professionals who may provide therapy include counselors, both at the Masters and Doctorate level, and many well-trained social workers and clerics. There are many overlaps in how we provide evaluation, diagnosis and therapy to our patients.

My sons used to tell me that if you don't know where you are going, any road will get you there. Even if you think you know where you are going, there may be different ways of getting there and unexpected detours along the way. Most of us can think of several routes from home to our place of work. Which one we take may depend on our mood, traffic flow, or other variables. If we need to pick up a loaf of bread on the way, we might choose an entirely new route. Therapy often offers the same options. Some therapists are better with one method than others and tend to use that one more frequently or exclusively.

If there were options, I would sometimes tell a new patient that there were several methods we might employ to reach the goal they wanted to achieve. I would then outline the varied approaches. I also explained why I might choose one method rather than another and asked their own preferences.

With so much information available from magazine articles, television and the internet, many patients came to me already expecting one approach, or they had fixed ideas about what therapy was like. Often I had to explain that I had no couch, might not be interested in their dreams, and had no instant advice to magically cure them in one session. Some patients expected me to utilize the "latest methods" being promoted on TV and in magazines. I sometimes had to tell them that even though I would do my best, I might not be able to help them at all. If pushed too hard to predict a cure, I would only say that Pixie Dust is always reserved for the final session. Most of them understood the humor of this.

I began my career with a psychodynamic orientation to therapy, but over the years I depended much less on any specific method or theory. I most frequently just engaged the client in a conversation similar to one among friends. Of course, if I listened well, their concerns always presented themselves. It seemed that this method, or rather seeming lack of method, worked quite as well, as any heavy-handed set of theories and interpretations. If I did not hear something important the first time, they always repeated it enough so I finally "got it."

# B.   Alexander's Rules of the Road

I have collected a few quips, hints and helpful stories that have been useful to me during my career as a practicing psychologist. I apologize in advance for any undocumented "stolen" material; these are all in common usage and, as far as I know, in the public domain. The paraphrases, misquotes, and out-and-out corny comments are probably entirely mine. Over the years I have frequently shared these with students. A few students have told me years later they would sometimes remember them at crucial times, and they worked! Some of these are already incorporated in the text, but I thought they were good enough to repeat. Feel free to "steal" them yourself if you like.

- If you do not know where you are going, any road will get you there.

- All behavior is over determined. (Freud) *My advice: Memorize this one!*

- The key to therapy is to interpret the resistance.

- Do not try to solve today's problems with yesterday's solutions.

- If you wonder whether you should do or say something with a patient, ask if you would do it if a colleague was there; better yet, when in doubt have a colleague there.

- Patients will never "get" your most brilliant insights or interventions, but years later they will credit you with curing them with something you never said.

- Being an Introject is not all bad.

- Geographic cures don't work. Everywhere you look, there you still are.

- Some clients ARE boring at times.

- When in doubt, trust your gut.

- A client with a history of more than three different, major psychiatric diagnoses probably has a borderline personality disorder.

- You should never be working harder than the client.

- Never do for someone what they can do for themselves.

- Remember on whose back the monkey entered the room.

  Or,

- The patient is the one who came in with the problem.

- When seeking Truth, Ockham's razor is a useful tool. (Also known as Root Cause Analysis or "Neti-Neti")

- A good presenting problem will get you in the door.

- *Primum non nocere.* First do no harm.

- Withhold Pixie Dust until the last session.

- Most theories fit nicely in a Procrustean bed.

- My family and friends often said they wished they knew the wonderful person my patients told them about.

- Do not participate in achieving a Pyrrhic Victory.

- Some people hold on to their problems because they have become their identity. Consider what they would have to face without them.

- Everyone has secrets. Even you.

- You do not need to have the problem in order to solve it.

- If you do not know where you are going, how will you lead the way?

- The best solution is the one that works.

- If you do not hear it the first time, the client will say it more often and louder until you do.

- So many theories; so few truths.

- Regarding cure rates: There are lies, there are damn lies, and then there are statistics.

- Freud may not have been right, but he was not wrong either.

- Trust but verify.

- It is not about you.

- All of us are sometimes voyeurs; some of us admit it.

- Your sexual interest in a client need not be an impediment to therapy, but neither is it a sign from God.

- Every good therapist has sometimes wished there was someone there who knew what they were doing.

- You do not need to have all the answers, but it helps to stay one step ahead of the patient.

- Consultant: A person from elsewhere who wears a suit, earns more than you do and probably makes the same recommendations you did, but they are seen as brilliant and are usually implemented.

- When you try to treat yourself, you have a fool for a patient.

- *De gustibus non est disputandum.* It is another's taste not yours. Leave it alone.

- NO ONE cares more about you than you do.

- Judge not lest ye be not judged.

- Maybe you haven't done this but you might have.

- Taking credit is always stolen credit. Return it to its rightful owner.

## C.   A Few Paraphrased Quotes from Literature

- "There is no such thing as good or evil. Nothing is itself virtuous or shameful, just or unjust, pleasant or painful, good or bad. Only our opinions give qualities to things, as salt gives savor to meats." "Everyone is equally incapable of doing evil or doing good. Good and evil exist only in the opinion we and others have of them." (Anatole France, *Thaïs*)

- "As long as we are what we are, we shall never find anything but our thoughts in the thoughts of others." (John Steinbeck)

- "There ain't no sin and there ain't no virtue. There's just stuff people do. It's all part of the same thing. Some of the things folks do are nice, and some are not nice, but that's as far as anyone has a right to say." (John Steinbeck, *Grapes of Wrath*)

- "Death is not the greatest loss in life. The greatest loss is what dies inside us while we live." (Norman Cousins)

- "Selfishness is not living as one wishes to live, it is asking others to live as one wishes to live." (Oscar Wilde, *The Soul of Man and Prison Writings*)

- "From the brain, and the brain alone, arise our pleasures, joys, laughter and jests, as well as our sorrows, pain, grief and tears." (Hippocrates)

- "Crying is alright while it lasts. But sooner or later you have to stop and then you still have to decide what to do." (C.S. Lewis, "The Silver Chair" from *The Chronicles of Narnia*).

- I remember once reading a story in which a man was shot in the Civil War and this left a hole in the roof of his mouth. Whenever his ideas are challenged, he points to the hole as the incontrovertible proof that he is right.

*I believe that some patients also use this strategy.*

# THE END

# Acknowledgements

As I wrote this book so many patients I have cared for over the years came to mind. To those of you whose story is not told here: You filled my memory and crowded my thoughts hoping to be acknowledged. I do so here. Know that I still think of you as well as those about whom I have written. And most importantly, a personal note to any patient of mine who might read this book: I appreciate the trust you placed in me. I enjoyed the opportunity to know you in a way that probably few others have. I hope that you benefited from our meeting and that wherever you are in life, you are doing well. Know that I am too.

I honor all the professors, supervisors and mentors who have tried to implant some wisdom in me, especially those who by teaching the art of psychotherapy to hundreds of students have helped thousands of people. I have tried to be as good a therapist and a teacher as they have been.

Most of all: My thanks and love goes to Diane Echols who has been my companion, soul mate and friend for more than ten years. She has put up with a lot of my craziness and has encouraged me to write this book. By frequent edits she improved the writing and saved me from a number of embarrassing errors. My apologies for the great meals she prepared that I missed in my obsession to work "just a little longer," and for the cups of coffee and kisses that kept me going.

And to the other people who helped me edit this book, correct my mistakes, improve my perceptions, and make it readable: Thank You.

www.ingramcontent.com/pod-product-compliance
Lightning Source LLC
Chambersburg PA
CBHW072120270326
41931CB00010B/1615